PURSUING DESTINY AGAINST THE ODDS

ARCHIE L. MCINNIS, II
CYNTHIA MCINNIS

Foreword by
WANZA LEFTWICH

Copyright © 2020 by Archie L. McInnis, II and Cynthia McInnis

All rights reserved. This book or any portion thereof may not be reproduced or used in any manner whatsoever without the express written permission of the publisher except for the use of brief quotations in a book review.

Printed in the United States of America

ISBN 978-1-7338592-1-9

BALM2 Productions, Inc

Brooklyn, NY

www.effect900.com

This collaboration is dedicated to my Great Aunt Jessie Mae Sivills, who was quintessential to the shaping of my motivation to succeed. My wife shares this sentiment, as her regular conversations with Aunt Jessie left a lasting and indelible mark in her heart.

CONTENTS

Acknowledgments — vii
Foreword — ix
Introduction — xi

PART I
HIS INSIGHT

1. A Good Report — 3
2. God's Timing — 9
3. Breaking Free (from a slave to a warrior) — 14
4. The Wilderness: A Wild, Homeless, Uncultivated State — 19
5. No Gain Without A Fight — 25
6. Find it, Stone it, and Burn it — 31
7. Rematch — 39
8. Legacy Minded — 44
9. Put Your Foot On Its Neck — 49
10. A Winner's Heart — 53

PART II
HER PERSPECTIVE

11. A Good Report — 59
12. God's Timing — 64
13. Breaking Free: From A Slave to a Warrior — 70
14. The Wilderness — 75
15. No Gain Without a Fight — 80
16. Find it, Stone it, Burn it — 84
17. Re-match — 90
18. Legacy Minded — 93
19. Put Your Foot on Its Neck — 99
20. A Winner's Heart — 103

ACKNOWLEDGMENTS

We would like to acknowledge the editing and design contributions of Executive Pastor, Wanza Leftwich, and Adrienne Horn.

FOREWORD

Who knew that the young girl in the brown and cream choir robe from the visiting church would marry the preacher's son who played the drums? From choir anniversaries to building churches and businesses, this dynamic duo had no idea that God orchestrated a life plan that the good Bishop or beautiful LadyDocta could deny.

It is one thing to have passion and purpose, but it is another to have faith to pursue your purpose in every stage of your life. Mistakenly, most have deemed destiny to be a one-time event, a culmination, or some heightened place of grandeur in life. Not so. Destiny is a series of occurrences prompted by the sovereign will of God for your life's path. You *live out* your destiny.

Pursuing Destiny Against the Odds is a biblically sound and dynamic collaboration of *His Insight* and *Her Perspective* on how to secure strategies for success by remaining in constant pursuit of the will of God for your life. This book extends

FOREWORD

beyond the cliché, often overly used, churchy vibration of the word destiny to demonstrating how to participate in the plans and purpose of God by activating your faith.

Nearly thirty years ago, when I went with Bishop and Lady-Docta on their first date, I had no idea that I would have a front-row experience on their destiny track. I have seen the tears and the pain, but more importantly, I have seen the constant miraculous victories that outweigh the suffering. I am particularly grateful to see their faith in action daily. Faith is their reality. Faith is their lifestyle.

When God saw that young man playing the drums and that young girl singing in the choir, He saw their family, their church with multiple locations that would serve thousands of people and impact generations, their businesses, and so much more. As a matter of fact, when God saw them, He saw you reading this book.

Perhaps your life has not been everything you have wanted it to be. Now is your time to change it. The principles written in this book will help you live the life you have been waiting to live. Hold them in your heart, meditate on them, and then act.

A life filled with success is not an illusion when you have a blueprint. This is it. Pursue your destiny against the odds.

Wanza Leftwich
Executive Pastor
Full Effect Gospel Ministries

INTRODUCTION

We have never written a book together until now. August 2021 will make 30 years of marriage, and we definitely have some stories to tell. Pastoring and being business partners has had its major ups and downs. The struggle has been real, but through faith and perseverance, we're still standing.

We've seen amazing results by stepping out on faith. Many things we had no pattern for; just an unction of the Holy Spirit and a desire to succeed. We are big dreamers, and we're not afraid to say it. Nothing happens without desire (Mark 11:24). Dreams do come to pass; you just have to be relentless in your pursuit of them.

Cynthia McInnis and I still have the same drive and passion after so many years of being together. We believe that the best is still yet to come. So we're determined to pursue destiny against the odds.

PART I
HIS INSIGHT
By Bishop Archie L. McInnis, II

CHAPTER 1
A GOOD REPORT

A good report eases the mind and brings peace to a troubled heart. The Bible says, "let not your heart be troubled, Ye believe in God believe also in me..." In times of trouble, we faint at heart because of whose report we chose to believe. What we believe determines our state of mind and the choices that we make. If you do not believe that you can do a thing, then you will not even make an effort to try it. Believing is the key that unlocks the door to limitless possibilities.

Presently, I am the senior pastor of one church in four states and an entrepreneur of a few small businesses. In 2005 I left a good-paying, secure city job with great benefits because I sensed God telling me to go into ministry full time. Fear gripped me. In my mind, I could never see that working. Me in full-time ministry? I questioned myself repeatedly. Why? Because in my mind, I had never seen it done before. I knew a few pastors who were in full-time ministry, but most of them either were retired from their job or were injured on their job and retired early on disability. I did not have a model before me to pattern. I had a wife and three small children to provide for, and I couldn't see myself surviving without my good secure job.

You must understand, to have a city job living in New York City was the way to go. You were set. Your life was secure with a city job. If you went to work every day, it would be a guarantee that you and your family would be well taken care of. So, for me to leave that job, I would be crazy. On top of that, I was graced to have such a good secure city job with the NYC department of sanitation, being that I have a B felony for Attempted Robbery, a dumb decision I made in high school hanging out with the wrong crowd.

I was charged like an adult and sentenced to 1 to 3 years. That one mistake had closed many doors for me growing up and still follows me today. Now, you understand why this job was a good job for me. What if I left this job and destroyed my only chance of a decent life? I was frantic in my mind and spirit. I said to myself, "I'm not leaving this job."

I stayed two more years until something happened. On the job, the bosses respected me, at least for the most part. Everyone knew that I was a pastor, so I was trusted as a man of God. But one day, things changed. The respect and favor that I had received on the job turned into a sense of hostility and dislike. I felt so deeply about it that it caused me to pray about it. And when I inquired to the Lord about it, He clearly said, "I told you to leave this job two years ago."

I wept because my disbelief had put me in a state of disharmony, not only to myself but to others. Like Jonah, I should have never been on that ship going down to Joppa when God

CHAPTER 1
A GOOD REPORT

A good report eases the mind and brings peace to a troubled heart. The Bible says, "let not your heart be troubled, Ye believe in God believe also in me…" In times of trouble, we faint at heart because of whose report we chose to believe. What we believe determines our state of mind and the choices that we make. If you do not believe that you can do a thing, then you will not even make an effort to try it. Believing is the key that unlocks the door to limitless possibilities.

Presently, I am the senior pastor of one church in four states and an entrepreneur of a few small businesses. In 2005 I left a good-paying, secure city job with great benefits because I sensed God telling me to go into ministry full time. Fear gripped me. In my mind, I could never see that working. Me in full-time ministry? I questioned myself repeatedly. Why? Because in my mind, I had never seen it done before. I knew a few pastors who were in full-time ministry, but most of them either were retired from their job or were injured on their job and retired early on disability. I did not have a model before me to pattern. I had a wife and three small children to provide for, and I couldn't see myself surviving without my good secure job.

You must understand, to have a city job living in New York City was the way to go. You were set. Your life was secure with a city job. If you went to work every day, it would be a guarantee that you and your family would be well taken care of. So, for me to leave that job, I would be crazy. On top of that, I was graced to have such a good secure city job with the NYC department of sanitation, being that I have a B felony for Attempted Robbery, a dumb decision I made in high school hanging out with the wrong crowd.

I was charged like an adult and sentenced to 1 to 3 years. That one mistake had closed many doors for me growing up and still follows me today. Now, you understand why this job was a good job for me. What if I left this job and destroyed my only chance of a decent life? I was frantic in my mind and spirit. I said to myself, "I'm not leaving this job."

I stayed two more years until something happened. On the job, the bosses respected me, at least for the most part. Everyone knew that I was a pastor, so I was trusted as a man of God. But one day, things changed. The respect and favor that I had received on the job turned into a sense of hostility and dislike. I felt so deeply about it that it caused me to pray about it. And when I inquired to the Lord about it, He clearly said, "I told you to leave this job two years ago."

I wept because my disbelief had put me in a state of disharmony, not only to myself but to others. Like Jonah, I should have never been on that ship going down to Joppa when God told him to go to Nineveh. It was Jonah's disobedience to the voice of God that caused a storm to hit the ship that he was on. To bring harmony to the ship and the waters, the people had to throw Jonah overboard. When God tells you to move, you got to move. A whole generation of people died in the wilderness because they chose to believe the report of the ten spies and not the report of the two spies, which were Joshua and Caleb.

Whose report you believe is detrimental to the trajectory of your life. I did not leave that job when God told me to because I believed the report of my fears and failures. Fear only shows you your weakness, never your strengths. Fear shows you defeat, never victory. Failure is a reference to your past mistakes, which constantly reminds you of your weaknesses. But faith enables you to see limitless possibilities allowing you to rise and succeed beyond your failures.

The ten spies brought back an evil report. The land flowed with milk and honey. The land was a prosperous land, and they even brought back a cluster of grapes to prove it. The cluster of grapes was so large that it took two men to carry it (Numbers 13:23). But because of the giants that were in the land, the ten spies saw it impossible for them to conquer the land. Leaving my job to go into full-time ministry was a giant for me. I only saw how small I was and not how big my God is. The giants were a problem for the ten spies. They could not get over how small they saw themselves compared to the giants.

The ten (spies) believed the report of self, meaning they only compared the giants to themselves and not to their God. Self is limited and cannot do the impossible. To do the impossible, you have to look beyond yourself (with God, all things are possible). When you only have yourself to look to, you can see the limitations to your abilities. But when you look to God and depend on His strength, you will see that there is no limitation to His power. We are to be strong in the Lord and in the power of His might (Ephesians 6:10).

Caleb and Joshua believed God and brought back a good report saying, "We are well able. Let us go up at once to possess it; for we are well able to overcome it" (Numbers 13:30). They believed that God had given them the land and that God would fight for them. "The Lord your God which goeth before you, he shall fight for you, according to all that he did for you in Egypt before your eyes;" (Deuteronomy 1:30).

Believing makes the difference between whether you stay in the wilderness or fight your way into the Promised Land. If you believe that you cannot, then you will not, but if you believe that you can with God, then you will.

Believe only. It does not matter how big or strong the opposition you face looks like. Choose to obey God and overcome every hindrance in your life. Fear gave the ten spies and the unbelieving Israelites a permanent address in the wilderness. They never experienced the true freedom that God wanted for them. They were physically free from Egypt, but their minds were still in bondage because of unbelief. They saw the Red Sea open like a highway with their own eyes. Then they witnessed it close back up and swallow Pharaoh's army. Yet, they still struggled to believe that God was with them. The problem here is that the children of Israel came out of Egypt on Moses's faith and not their own faith.

Perhaps some of us made it this far because of someone else using their faith for us. But to go into the land of promise that flows with milk and honey, you have got to use your own faith.

Only the believers made it into the Promised Land. I call them the Generation of Faith. Joshua and Caleb believed when the ten spies did not believe. I believe that because the ten spies' report was the majority out of the twelve that Moses sent to spy out the land that the children of Israel believed them over Joshua and Caleb's good report.

There were more people telling me to stay on my job and retire than there were people encouraging me to obey the voice of God. The twelve that Moses used to spy out the land were chief leaders of the twelve tribes of Israel. They were important men of high esteem and influential in their individual tribes. These men were taken seriously. Their evil report of fear and unbelief spread through the camp of Israel like a wildfire. Sometimes the truth is not in the majority.

It was the majority that chose Barabbas over Jesus, the Way, the Truth, and the Life (John 14:6), even when Pilate could not find anything to accuse Jesus of (Luke 23:14). Sometimes men of great esteem and influence can be blinded to the truth. Because the children of Israel received that lie from the ten, I call their report a lie because the truth is that they were able to possess the land. Their lack of right believing destroyed their destiny to the Promised Land. They believed a lie rather than receiving the truth. That lie, that evil report of fear, killed them in the wilderness (Number 14:23). Everyone twenty years and older died in the wilderness without entering the Promised Land.

Joshua and Caleb were the only ones of Moses's generation that lived to see the Promised Land (Numbers 14:38). In this narrative, the two men (spies) believed they were greater than the ten men (spies) that did not believe. Faith is an unstoppable force that defies the odds. Faith is supernatural. Faith is trusting the Word of God, no matter what. When most said that I was crazy for thinking about leaving my job at the New York City Department of Sanitation, there was one that believed with me, my wife, Cynthia. She was my Caleb. She stood with me and concurred that God had released me into full-time ministry.

Every Joshua needs a Caleb. It was Caleb that assisted Joshua in that great journey of faith into the Promised Land. When I told my wife that God told me to leave that job, she received it as a good report and said obey God. She could see me doing better without that job. She saw me doing more for God and the ministry. She saw us expanding the ministry because I would now have more time to do what God had called me to do. Oh, it was a good report. I began to forget about the giants that I would face and started focusing on the grapes. In other words, I began to focus on the possibilities, the good things that the Lord had for me and my wife. I knew that God would not leave us but would fight for us if we obeyed His voice.

Today it has been over fifteen years now that I have been in full-time ministry, and we have never lacked anything. God has been our sustainer. He provided everything that the job gave me and more from healthcare to our own Roth IRA. Now that is a good report. Because we dared to trust God, we have seen His faithfulness towards us. Whenever God shows you your destiny, believe it, move towards it, and possess it regardless of the giants that are already there.

CHAPTER 2
GOD'S TIMING

One of the most difficult things, I think, is to know God's timing. It is easy to know God's timing after He has done a thing, but it is not easy to know when He is going to do a thing. From the creation of the world to the birth of Christ, even the return of Christ (Mathew 24:36). Who could know the exact time for when God decided or decides to move, create, or plan purpose?

We know the seasons winter, spring, summer, and fall. We know by a child's age whether they should be in nursery, kindergarten, first grade, etc. We know what time to be at work, lunchtime, dinner time, etc. Perhaps even you know when it is time for a change in your life, and that is something that you cannot always explain but sense. Like when it is time to retired from being single and find a spouse or sense that it is time for a closer relationship with God. Or to take your business or career to the next level. But most times, I discovered in our walk with God that God's timing has much to do with His plans for our lives, not our plans for our lives. "Many are the plans in a person's heart, but it is the Lord's purpose that prevails" (Proverbs 19:21). Plans and purpose are equal to time. When God plans your life, He plans it according to His purpose, and nothing happens without purpose or before it is time.

In the book of Esther, there was a plot to destroy the Jewish nation, but God orchestrated their deliverance through a Jewish girl named Esther. Esther was chosen to be the king's new wife after his present wife, Queen Vashti, refused him. The king was incredibly angry and took counsel from his advisors on what was to be done to Vashti. It was agreed upon that Vashti should be banished from the presence of the king and that a new wife should be chosen that is more worthy than she. God's perfect timing caused Vashti to be deposed and Esther to be exposed.

Esther became the king's wife but concealed that she was a Jewish girl. Haman's plot to kill the Jews failed because of God's strategic planning and timing. Once Esther revealed to the king her true identity and conveyed Haman's plan to kill her people, the king immediately saved his Queen's family and her nation. God set the hold thing up. He planned the year, date, and time that Esther should be born. The purpose of her life was to save a nation. "... who knoweth whether thou art come to the kingdom for such a time as this" (Esther 4:14)? God's purpose for Esther's life was perfectly planned and timed for her to be in the kingdom. Nothing happens before God's timing.

Lazarus was sick in John 11 and his sisters Mary and Martha called for Jesus to heal him. Jesus showed up after Lazarus was dead for four days. Did Jesus not care about

Lazarus? Of course, Jesus cared about him. While Lazarus's sisters wanted Jesus to heal him to prevent his death. Jesus wanted to wait until Lazarus was dead. See, God had a plan and purpose for Lazarus that was unknown to Lazarus's sisters, who were praying for him. Sometimes the will of God is not evident at the moment. Jesus had something greater in store for Lazarus. Something that would bring more glory to God.

Which is a greater miracle? To be sick and healed or to be dead and then raised from the dead? I presume, like me, you chose the latter. When there is life in the body, there is usually hope for recovery. People usually still pray for the sick but not for the dead. Once you are dead, it is over. You are eulogized, cried over, and buried. Then the people go home back to their lives. Because once you are dead, your existence in time is done.

Jesus raising Lazarus from the dead brought an even greater glory to God in the eyes of those who watched and even those who heard about the miracle. Also, many people came to see Jesus because of the miracle of Him raising Lazarus from the dead. In God's perfect timing, He purposely used Lazarus's demise for His own glory before the people.

In John 5, there is a certain man lame for thirty-eight years. The Bible says that Jesus knew that this man was in that case for a long time. With so many people trying to be healed at the pool of Bethesda, Jesus passed everyone and went to this certain man who the Bible does not name. The amazing thing is that Jesus knew this man's case.

I am encouraged to know that Jesus knows my every case. He knows every struggle and every battle that we face. Not only does He know, but He has a time and purpose to set us free. This man was lame for thirty-eight years. We do not know how old he was, but Jesus's public ministry began at the age of thirty, and His ministry on earth lasted thirty-three years.

God waited until Jesus was born and for Him to grow up before he met this lame man on a certain day to tell him to rise, take up thy bed and walk. I do not believe that Jesus meeting this man the day that He did was a coincidence. I believe that God had a purpose, planned the timing, and orchestrated the outcome. Jesus only did what the Father told Him to do. God is strategic. He is not trying to figure out a plan. He already had a plan for your life before He created you. God chose this certain lame man. Not just to heal him but to give him eternal life (John 5:14).

When we look at the life of Joshua, he was a man of faith. He believed God no matter how fearful the other ten were who Moses sent out to spy the land. Joshua and Caleb trusted God. Joshua, even though he was fearless, was also faithful. He followed Moses's instructions. Even though Joshua and Caleb had the faith to process the land, they did not have the authority to possess it. Moses and the children of Israel were at a standstill because the evil report from the ten spies out of the twelve that Moses sent out to spy out the land of promise put fear in all of the people. Because of that fear, God promised that none would enter the land of promise except Joshua, Caleb, and the new generation that God would raise up in the wilderness (Numbers 14).

So, Joshua had to wait on God's timing to enter the Promised Land. Because we have faith to do a thing does not mean that it is God's will for us to do it. Faith is knowing God's will and putting that faith to action towards what God has purposed for our lives. "Except the Lord build the house, they labour in vain that build it: except the Lord keep the city, the watchman waketh but in vain" (Psalms 127:1).

It is our job to discover the plan, purpose, and will of God for our lives. When we do that, we discover God's blueprint for our lives. If we knew God's blueprint for every intricate decision we made in our lives, we would prosper in everything we did (Psalm 1:3). Except the Lord build the house, we labor to build what God has already built for us. An architect puts the building on paper, and the contractor follows the architect's blueprint. God has already architected our lives. We just have to follow the blueprint, which is the Word of God, to succeed.

Through prayer and meditation on God's Word, He will give us revelation on what direction to take in every season of our lives. Joshua and Caleb knew that to be successful in conquering the Promised Land, they had to move in God's timing. Even though the Promised Land was for them to have according to God's will, they still had to move with God, not ahead of God. After Moses died and that faithless generation of twenty years and older died, God spoke to Joshua and said, "Now it is time to go over this Jordan" (Joshua 1). Because Joshua and Caleb moved in God's timing, they succeeded in conquering the land of promise, defeating every giant and enemy that stood in their way. When God is for you, who can be against you (Romans 8:31)?

Knowing God's Word and having a habitual lifestyle of prayer will position you to hear from God for the right time and season for every move you make. "In all thy ways acknowledge him, and he shall direct thy paths" (Proverbs 3:6).

CHAPTER 3

BREAKING FREE (FROM A SLAVE
TO A WARRIOR)

Joshua was born in Egypt and was probably the same age as Caleb, whom he was generally associated with. He witnessed all the events of the children of Israel coming out of Egypt and held the place as commander of the host of the Israelites at their battle against the Amalekites (Exodus. 17:8-16). He became Moses's minister and accompanied him part of the way when he went up to Mount Sinai to receive the two tables (Exodus 32:17). Under the direction of God, Moses, before his death, proclaimed Joshua publicly with authority over the people as his successor (Deuteronomy. 31:23).

Joshua was born a slave in Egypt; he was about forty years old at the time of their Exodus out of Egypt. His name was changed from Oshea to Jehoshua (Joshua), which means Jehovah is help (Numbers 13:16). And his name was the key to his life and work. He brought the people into Canaan through wars and in the distribution of the land among the tribes. Joshua was the embodiment of his name, Jehovah is help.

Joshua is a type of Christ (Hebrews 4:8) in the following ways:

1. In the name common to both
2. Joshua brings the people into the possession of the Promised Land, as Jesus brings his people to the heavenly Canaan
3. As Joshua succeeded Moses, the Gospel of Jesus Christ succeeds the Law

Joshua is an incredible example of breaking free from bondage and a slave mindset. Being born a slave under a hard taskmaster like Pharaoh and never knowing freedom until Moses, it seems so remarkable how he broke free from a slave mindset so quickly. I believe that it was his connection to Moses. Out of all the Israelites, Joshua was the one who followed Moses closely. In fact, as aforementioned, he became Moses's servant or minister.

Moses, even though he was born to a slave mother, was raised by a free Egyptian woman who happened to find baby Moses in a basket floating down the Nile River. Moses's natural mother could not hide him from the executioners who were killing all male children birthed by the Israelite women. The children of Israel were becoming so strong in number that the Egyptians began killing off the male children.

The ones who enslaved them knew that Israel was stronger than them, and if a war ever broke out, the Egyptians would be defeated. But Israel knew not their own strength. As a result,

Pharaoh's daughter, who found Moses in the Nile River, brought him into the palace and raised him as her own son. Moses was raised free, and his thinking was as a free man. When he discovered he was a Jew and not an Egyptian, he longed for his brethren to be free.

It became so bad one day that when he saw an Egyptian beating a Hebrew slave, Moses slew that Egyptian and buried him in the sand. Having a freedom mindset, Moses fought for his rights and the rights of his brethren. But Moses's deed angered Pharaoh and Moses fled Egypt for fear of his life. On his quest to make a new life for himself, he discovered the purpose and calling for his life.

It took Moses forty years to come into his calling. Imagine being physically free but in bondage mentally and spiritually. It was not until Moses turned eighty years old that he received a revelation from God for the purpose of his existence. All these years, he was living but not living in his purpose. I believe that's bondage. Nothing really major was happening for Moses after he fled from Egypt. At least in Egypt, he was a prince and lived a life of royalty and rulership as the grandson of Pharaoh. But fear made him flee Egypt when his purpose and calling was in Egypt. He discovered this forty years later after living a regular life, finding a wife, having children, and shepherding sheep for his father-in-law, Jethro.

His life became average until one day in the desert, he noticed a bush on fire that was not consumed by the fire. Lo and behold, the voice of the Lord spoke to him through that burning bush and revealed to him that he was to go back to Egypt to tell Pharaoh to "let my people go free." Amazing. The very place Moses ran from was the very place God was sending him back to. It was the very thing that he was born to do – free God's people from the bondage and enslavement of Egypt. Moses's desire to save the life of a Hebrew slave from being destroyed by an Egyptian was a sign of where his heart was.

Moses had a heart to fight for the freedom of his Hebrew brethren, who were slaves. He saved one Hebrew when he killed the Egyptian but feared that the Word would get back to Pharaoh. Imagine Moses gone forty years, but his heart is still for freeing his brethren and family from the bondage of Egypt. Imagine Moses for forty years living a seemly content life, but in heart, he wished that he could free his people. Moses was free physically, but, in his heart, he was a slave to fear. God knew what was in Moses's heart because it was God that put that desire there.

Therefore, the very thing Moses ran from God was sending him back to. If you are not doing what God has put in your heart, you are not free. Get free today, and do all that God has placed in your heart to do. When Moses freed the children of Israel out of bondage, he also freed himself. God was with him every step of the way because being a deliverer to God's people, the Jews, was God's calling and purpose for Moses's life. It was the very reason why Moses was born. Powerful.

I believe that that freedom of finally knowing his God-given purpose attracted Joshua to Moses. Faith is contagious (John 8:30). Moses spoke with power, and he walked in confidence and did many miracles in Egypt. Joshua, who was born a slave in Egypt, followed Moses closely and became his right-hand man. A slave became a warrior. You can only go as far as you can see, and you can only achieve as much as you believe. How you see yourself and what you believe about yourself determines the limitations that you will put on yourself. I believe that Joshua, seeing the unlimited power of God working through Moses, lit a fire in his spirit to believe that if God could work like that through Moses that He could work like that through him too if he believed.

There is no record of Joshua being a warrior in Egypt, but we see him in battle in Israel's first battle recorded outside of Egypt against the Amalekites. I believe God gave Joshua an anointing to become a great fighter. Moses gave Joshua his name after the battle with the Amalekites. As aforementioned, Joshua's name was Oshea, which means help. Joshua was a helper by nature. But when he started working with Moses, an anointing to war came on him, and Moses changed his name to Jehoshua (Joshua), which means Jehovah is help. God anointed Joshua because of his desire to be a helper. He became a great asset to Moses, and in time, Moses made him his minister, and then eventually, Moses proclaimed him to be his successor. This goes to show us that regardless of what your past has been, God can destroy every bondage in your life if you believe.

Fight for your freedom. Refuse to be a slave to fear and excuses. Become a great warrior like Joshua and a great deliverer like Moses and pursue your God-given purpose no matter the opposition. "For we walk by faith, not by sight" (2 Corinthians 5:7).

CHAPTER 4
THE WILDERNESS: A WILD, HOMELESS, UNCULTIVATED STATE

The wilderness was never supposed to be the permanent residence for the children of Israel, but for some of them, it became exactly just that. The wilderness was not just naturally uncultivated and wild without civil structure. It was also a typology of the disposition, mindset, and behavior of the masses of the children of Israel that came out of Egypt. They were free but not ready for the responsibility of their freedom. Like a wilderness, they were wild, undisciplined, and disregarded structure. Moses, their leader who led them out of Egypt, could not cultivate and free their minds from so many years of them having a slave mentality.

To be absolutely free, there must be a change of mind. People who are free physically but have the same slave mindset will repeat the same cycles, no matter where they go. Paul encourages us to have the mind of Christ (Philippians 2:5-11).

There cannot be true change in a person's life until that person receives the Word of God. True transformation is achieved by the renewing of the mind (Romans 12:2).

The children of Israel had experienced the delivering power of God. They saw the plaques come through Egypt, and they were not harmed because of God's protection. They saw how God opened the Red Sea and witnessed Pharaoh's army drown in that same Red Sea that they had just passed through on dry ground. They even rejoice with dancing and praises after God gave them the victory over Pharaoh and his army. But to experience the miracles was not enough to get them out of the wilderness. The miracles did not cultivate faith because if it did, they would have entered the land of promise. As I mentioned before, it was Moses's faith that God used to bring them out of Egypt (Hebrews 11:23-29).

Faith comes by hearing and hearing by the Word of God (Romans 10:17). Thy Word have I hid in my heart that I might not sin against thee (Psalms 119:11). The Word changes your heart, and as a man thinks in his heart, so is he (Proverbs 24:7). Not only does the Word change your heart, but as a man thinks in his heart, so is he in his behavior. What you meditate on develops your mindset. A word from the Lord turned Gideon from being a fearful man into a man of boldness, and he defeated his enemies (Judges 7).

The Word of God is an incorruptible seed. A seed grows and develops into its full potential. What is in the seed is in the tree. An orange seed can only produce oranges. So, a seed can only produce what is in it. So, when the Word of God is received like a seed, which the Bible says that the Word is a seed, you can produce all that the Word says you can have. When the Word is in your heart, miracles are in you, healing is in you, success is in you, and so much more (1 Peter 1:23).

Israel had an uncultivated mind even though they were out of the house of bondage. That slave mindset crippled their ability to see anything greater than where they came from. Their past became their handicap. They had no imagination for their future. They did not put the Word in their hearts. When you put God's Word in your heart, you will produce imagination, and imagination produces feelings, and feelings produce actions that bring forth fruit (Psalms 1).

An uncultivated mind is a mind that is not trained by God's Word (Romans 12:2). The wilderness is uncultivated only because it is not in a civilized development. In a civilized development, trees and grass are manicured. They are not allowed to grow wild and out of control. In other words, they are trained and cultivated how they should grow. The mind must be cultivated for there to be true transformation.

The children of Israel were known to be a stiff-necked people (Exodus 32:9). They refused to change. Just as it takes a man to till the ground or cultivate a garden, it takes someone to mentor and train you to become all that you can be. God used Moses to train and cultivate Israel, but they rebelled.

When a person is uncultured, it means that that person lacks in education or refinement. It means that they are growing or developing without a cultivator. Anybody can grow but to grow without proper cultivation is to grow wild like a wilderness. That is what the wilderness is; it is wild growth, uncultivated, undeveloped, with no one to till the ground. When you have no leader, mentor, or no one in your life to help train, educate, and renew your mind, you grow wild, out of control, and become undeveloped.

Everyone needs to be trained. Children, new hires, husbands, wives, first-time drivers. It takes training. There are rules and laws that govern countries, states, and cities. If you are uneducated with these rules and laws, it determines how well you succeed in life or not. And they are rules and laws that govern faith, and if you do not have faith, it is impossible to please God (Hebrews 11:6).

And it was Israel's very lack of faith that caused them to miss out on the Promised Land. God had to wait until a new generation was born, and for that old generation to die before they could enter the Promised Land. The old generation represents an old slave mindset, but the new generation represents a free man's mindset that says anything is possible. God was able to use that generation to enter the Promised Land.

There were pastures in the wilderness to feed Israel's sheep and cattle. God also provided mana to feed them, and when they could not find water, God provided them water from a rock. Yet, they lived in tents. Tents were meant for travelers to provide temporary shelter when needed. God wanted to provide them houses and land in Canaan, but their uncultivated, unbelieving hearts settled for living in tents. God wanted ownership for them, but they settled for tents. They were homeless in the wilderness. Provision does not mean that you stay permanently. God ordained for them to go through the wilderness, not to make the wilderness their home.

I remember starting our church in the basement of our home. People thought that I was crazy. I had a food pantry and the whole nine yards in our basement. Eventually, the church had taken over our whole house. I even had a professional sign on the outside of the front of the house. The sign read Full Effect Gospel Ministries, Inc (temporary location). I had the sign put up because I wanted people to know that a church was there, but also, I wanted them to know that church would be held there temporarily. I thought that it was important to mention the temporary location on the sign to indicate to people that we had a vision.

It is really not how you start off; it is how you finish. In eighteen months, the church was out of our house and in its own building. My wife and I made a choice to use our home for church services because we were thinking of ownership, not renting. In making that decision, we were able to purchase our first church building instead of renting. It was a great sacrifice, but that sacrifice became a great blessing to us and our church.

Never make anything temporary permanent. When God provides in a temporary place, it is only to sustain you until you get to your permanent destination. There was little war in the wilderness. Nobody fights wars to keep a wilderness or uncultivated place, and that made Israel comfortable. Wars are only fought for things of great value. And if you are afraid to fight for your promise, you will stay living in dry places, dreaming about what you could have had.

Once Israel's new generation made it to Canaan, the mana ceased. They did not have to wait for God to feed them. All they had to do was eat from the trees that bear fruit because they were now in the land that flowed with milk and honey, the land of promise. And that is what God wants for us, more than mana. He wants us to live the promise, not the process. Some of us just live the process, the struggle, and never come into the promise. But when we cultivate and train our minds with the knowledge of what God wants for us, we will never settle for a wilderness lifestyle, but we will pursue the promises of God against all odds.

CHAPTER 5
NO GAIN WITHOUT A FIGHT

Joshua had an amazing career of victories. He won many battles to possess the land of promise. Joshua defeated over thirty-one kings to possess the land of promise. The promise did not come without conflict. A good life does not come without a fight. It takes faith, prayer, and determination to have good success.

"This book of the law shall not depart out of thy mouth; but thou shalt meditate therein day and night, that thou mayest observe to do according to all that is written therein: for then thou shalt make thy way prosperous, and then thou shalt have good success" (Joshua 1:8).

Fighting the fight of faith is the key to achieving. Joshua had to believe to succeed. Faith was the motivating factor that compelled Joshua into the Promised Land. Remember, there were giants in Canaan, but Joshua believed that God had given him the land. See, if you do not believe, you will never even try to cross that Jordan River. Joshua and the new generation of

Israel had to cross the Jordan River before they could get to Jericho. The former generation some forty years earlier failed to go over Jordan. To be brought out of Egypt is one thing but to cross over the Jordan is where the rubber meets the road. If you do not have faith to cross the Jordan, you will never conquer Jericho. It took faith and courage to cross the Jordan River.

The Jordan represents those things that distract you from achieving your goals. It represents excuses on why you cannot do a thing. There were no enemies stopping Israel at the Jordan. Their enemies were in Jericho. Their challenge was to defeat personal fear and believe that if God said go over this Jordan, they would be able to do it with His help. If you never cross over Jordan, you will never possess the promise (Joshua 1:11). Joshua says that we shall pass over this Jordan to possess the land, which the Lord your God gives to you to possess it. We shall go over this Jordan.

I believe that before you can really live in the promises of God, you have to get over some things that are in your way. Jordan was in their way of possessing the land. What has been hindering you from possessing the land of promise? What is in your way? Anything that hinders you from reaching your destiny is a Jordan in your life. I encourage you to go over that Jordan. I even encourage you to get over that Jordan. Sometimes past hurts and disappointments hinder you from moving forward. Un-forgiveness blocks your spiritual flow and harmony with the Lord (Mark 11:25). Before you can fight the enemy without, you must contend with the enemy within.

Jordan represents personal fears and insecurities. It represents how you see yourself and what you believe about yourself.

The way to conquer your fears and insecurities is by knowing that your identity is in Christ Jesus, our Lord. We were chosen in Christ before the foundation of the world. We have been predestined by God in Jesus Christ, according to the good pleasure of His will, to be the praise of the glory of His grace, where He has accepted us in the beloved.

Read Ephesians Chapter 1. We were chosen in Christ, meaning that we belong to Him, and God has given us a purpose in Christ. It is the reason for our existence. So, our identity is in Christ. It is in Him we live, move, and have our being. I can do all things through Christ that strengthens me. Paul said it is not I but Christ that lives in me.

We have been predestined by God in Christ Jesus. Our destiny is in Christ by the will of God. So, if our destiny is in Christ, then we look to him to lead the way in our lives. We win in Christ, we have the victory in Christ, and we are never defeated in Christ. Our identity is in an undefeated champion – Jesus Christ. When you know that, your thinking changes because now you see yourself the way God sees you. And when God sees you, He sees the Christ in you, which is His beloved son.

In Ephesians, God calls us His beloved. Beloved means greatly loved, dear to the heart. We are greatly loved and dear to God's heart just as Jesus is because our identity is in Christ Jesus. When God sees us, He sees Jesus (of course, only if you have accepted Jesus Christ as your Lord and Savior). God loved and chose Abraham to be the vehicle for which Jesus Christ would come through his bloodline. God told Abraham, whoever blesses you and your seed, I will bless. Whoever curses you and your seed, I will curse. "And I will bless them that bless thee, and curse him that curseth thee: and in thee shall all families of the earth be blessed" (Genesis 12:3).

The children of Israel are the seed of Abraham. Their identity was in Abraham, who is the Father of Faith. The promises of God were on the bloodline of Abraham's children (seed). So, God would bless whoever blessed Israel, but whoever cursed Israel God would curse. If the children of Israel understood their identity, they would have never walked in fear. They would have walked by faith, knowing that the God of Abraham would fight for them. Even we Christians today should know that if we belong to Christ Jesus, then we also are Abraham's children and have the same exact promises as the children of Israel. "And if ye be Christ's, then are ye Abraham's seed, and heirs according to the promise" (Galatians 3:29). Whoever blesses you, God will bless. Whoever curses you, God will curse. God will fight for you only believe.

One thing is important to know, and that is just because God fights for you does not mean that you do not do your part. Nothing of great value comes without conflict. Conflict is proof that you are headed in the right direction. There is no change without discomfort. Jesus said, if you suffer with me, you shall reign with me. Most want to reign and gain without any pain, but the truth is there is no gain without a fight. We must endure hardness as a good soldier. We must fight the good fight of faith. Hell is against us and will try to block our progress. Jesus said, "... upon this rock I will build my church; and the gates of hell shall not prevail against it" (Matthew 16:18).

We are the church of Jesus Christ, and the gates of hell will not stop us. The purpose of gates is to control who goes in or out. What place mainly has gates? Prisons. The devil wants to keep us as prisoners. Hell's gates are designed to keep the believers boxed in, prevented from progress like Pharaoh kept the children of Israel in bondage. But God broke those gates down by using Moses to set His people free. Gates are not just iron or steel, but gates are mental blocks that prevent you from seeing possibilities. If we see our identity in Christ Jesus, Hell will not be able to prevail against us.

Jesus completed His assignment on the earth regardless of the oppositions He faced, and so will you. Know that we have been blessed with all spiritual blessings in heavenly places in Christ (Ephesians 1:3). Take note that the Scripture does not say that we will be blessed with all spiritual blessings in heavenly places in Christ. It says that we have been blessed with all spiritual blessings in heavenly places in Christ, meaning that we are already blessed with all spiritual blessings. Not going to be, but we already are. That is powerful. Not only are we blessed with all spiritual blessings, but they are in heavenly places. Heaven is fighting for you. Heaven is providing for you; heaven is on your side. You cannot be defeated.

Also, we are blessed in heavenly places in Christ. We are in Christ. Our identity is in Him; we are with Him in heavenly places. We are one with Christ. In covenant, two or more become one. Paul gives us an example of Christ and His church being one as when a man marries a woman, they become one (Ephesians 5:25-32). He is in us, and we are in Him. So, when we loose and bind, the heaven does it with us. "And I will give unto thee the keys of the kingdom of heaven: and whatsoever thou shalt bind on earth shall be bound in heaven: and whatsoever thou shalt loose on earth shall be loosed in heaven" (Matthew 16:19).

When you live knowing your identity in Christ, you know that you have all you need in you to win every battle that you will face. The Christ in you shall never be defeated, and He never ran, and he never will. Christ lives in you, and you can do all things through Christ that strengthens you. Fulfill your God-given destiny, no matter the cost. You will have to fight but know God is fighting with you, and you will win. There is no gain without a fight, so become one who loves to fight. It took Joshua seven years of war to conquer the land of Canaan, but without fail, he took the whole land. God wants you to take all of what He has promised you. Do not settle for the incomplete and almost. Instead, take it all like Joshua because all that God promised you is yours. Pursue destiny against the odds. God will fight with you.

CHAPTER 6
FIND IT, STONE IT, AND BURN IT

There was a woman in the Bible caught in the act of adultery. She was brought before Jesus by the Scribes and Pharisees so that they might try to trap him into saying something that they could use against him. It was the Law of Moses that the punishment for the sin of adultery was stoning. Even though this act of sin was to trap Jesus and had really nothing to do with the woman, she was exposed and brought to shame because of her sin. "Godliness makes a nation great, but sin is a disgrace to any people" (Proverbs 14:34).

Sin brings shame and is a reproach. Reproach is to find fault, discredit, and disapprove. That is really what the Scribes and Pharisees were trying to do to Jesus. They were trying to find fault that they could use to discredit and disapprove him. And that is what the enemy does; he uses sin to discredit and disapprove a person. Once a person falls into sin, credibility and trust become an issue. People tend to lose their influence once they have fallen from grace.

It was the enemy's plot to trap Jesus. Consequently, the people would find fault in Him. But Jesus, in His wisdom, stooped down and wrote on the ground as though He heard them not. I think that He needed a moment to think of how He should handle this complicated situation. A woman's life was on the line, as well as His credibility. He needed a God-given response to their question. It's not recorded in the scriptures what He wrote on the ground, but when he rose from the ground, he said to them, "He that is without sin among you, let him first cast a stone at her." Absolutely an astounding response.

Jesus's answer brought conviction to them so that the men dropped their rocks. Now the woman was free from her accusers, and her life was saved from being stoned to death. What a merciful and kind Lord is our Jesus. But something interesting happens. Jesus says to the woman, "Go and sin no more." Huh? Is that possible? *Go and sin no more.* Sounds like an impossible thing, but I believe that Jesus would never tell you to do anything that you could not do. Besides that, it was her sin of adultery that put her in the spotlight of disgrace.

She probably thought that no one knew of her life of adultery. But when the Scribes and Pharisees wanted to find a way to discredit Jesus, they used this woman's indiscretions. It is a mistake to assume that only you know your secret sin, especially when it is a sin that includes another person in the act. Either someone sees you when you think not, or perhaps the one you committed the sin with opens their mouth about it to impress someone that they assume will keep their secret. Who really knows how this woman's secret got out and where was the man that committed the sin with her? However, the Scriptures say that your sin will find you out (Numbers 32:23). Sin eventually exposes and brings shame to your life, even death (Romans 6:23). Jesus was trying to prevent future shame and disgrace for the woman caught in adultery by telling her to go and sin no more.

Sin is dangerous because sin is the opposite of God's best for us. Adam and Eve lost the Garden of Eden because of sin. The Garden of Eden was a place of peace and prosperity. There was no lack, sickness, poverty, or even death in the garden. When sin entered their lives, so did every curse that comes with sin. In John 5, the lame man that I mentioned in chapter two was lame because of a habitual life of sin. He was not born lame; he became lame.

Jesus told the lame man after he was made whole to "go and sin no more lest a worse thing comes upon you" (John 5:14). Sin no more means stop sinning. It was his sin that produced his impotence in his legs. Sin means disobedience to the laws of God. We do not know what kind of life of sin the lame man lived, but we do know for ourselves that immoral lifestyles cause diseases. AIDS, venereal diseases, diabetes, cancer, and other diseases are not just hereditary. Some of the causes of these diseases come from life choices.

Gluttony is a sin. Being overweight can cause all kinds of health issues. Cigarette smoking causes cancer. Yet people still smoke anyway. Unprotected sex and sex without marriage risk not only your health but also having children out of wedlock that can add other generational family issues. Whenever we disobey God's law, we can expect life-threatening issues. Now we know that the law came by Moses, but grace and truth came by Jesus Christ. However, if Jesus Christ, who is Grace, tells you to stop sinning lest a worse thing comes upon you, it is best that you take heed. I believe that grace not only forgives you of sin but also teaches you how to prevent a life of sin.

Daniel had an excellent spirit and prospered in a Babylonian country when Israel was in exile. Instead of adapting to their Babylonian gods and culture, he lived a clean life before God, and no evil that befell him could consume him (Daniel 6). Evil can befall you, but it does not mean that it will consume you. Job was a perfect and upright man, one that feared God and eschewed evil. He was not consumed by the evil things that happened to him (The Book of Job). Job waited on the Lord to turn his situation around, and when He did, Job received double for his trouble. There are benefits that come with obedience. "If they obey and serve him, they shall spend their days in prosperity, and their years in pleasures" (Job 36:11). And there are consequences to disobedience. "But if they obey not, they shall perish by the sword, and they shall die without knowledge" (Job 36:12).

When Joshua and the children of Israel conquered Jericho by an amazing miracle of Jericho's wall falling down, God gave them specific instructions on what to do upon their entrance into the city. "Jericho and everything in it must be completely destroyed as an offering to the Lord. Only Rahab, the prostitute, and the others in her house will be spared, for she protected our spies. "Do not take any of the things set apart for destruction, or you yourselves will be completely destroyed, and you will bring trouble on the camp of Israel. Everything made from silver, gold, bronze, or iron is sacred to the Lord and must be brought into his treasury" (Joshua 6:17-19).

Joshua and Israel conquered Jericho in a miraculous way.

Their victory was astounding. They were instructed to destroy everything as an offering until the Lord except for Rahab, the harlot, and her family because she protected the spies that Joshua sent to spy out the land. Also, the silver, gold, bronze, and iron were sacred to the Lord and to be put into the treasury. "But Israel violated the instructions about the things set apart for the Lord. A man named Achan had stolen some of these dedicated things, so the Lord was very angry with the Israelites. Achan was the son of Carmi, a descendant of Zimri son of Zerah, of the tribe of Judah" (Joshua 7:1).

One man's disobedience put all of Israel in jeopardy. They had a massive victory in Jericho, but that was just the beginning. They had much more territory to conquer. The next city on their list to conquer was Ai. Because Ai was a smaller city much smaller than that of Jericho, Joshua took fewer men into battle. They just knew that they would defeat the people of Ai with ease, but they were in for a rude awakening.

The men of Ai defeated Joshua and his men badly. Joshua was in disarray, shocked and saddened by their defeat by such a small group of people compared to the city of Jericho. Joshua fell to the ground upon his face feeling rejected and forsaken by God. But God spoke to Joshua and told him to get up; there was sin in the camp. One man's sin caused Israel to be defeated in a battle that they were clearly supposed to win. "For as by one man's disobedience many were made sinners, so by the obedience of one shall many be made righteous" (Romans 5:19). The action of one can affect many. It can either hurt you or help you. Sin can affect generations passing from one generation to the next (Deuteronomy 5:9).

Blessings are also generational. "That in blessing I will bless thee, and in multiplying I will multiply thy seed as the stars of the heaven, and as the sand which is upon the seashore; and thy seed shall possess the gate of his enemies; And in thy seed shall all the nations of the earth be blessed; because thou hast obeyed my voice" (Genesis 22:17-18).

For Joshua to get back on a winning streak in conquering the land of promise, he had to deal with the sin within the camp. Sin was hindering their winning flow. Joshua searched the camp and found Achan to be guilty of disobedience unto the Lord. Because of this sin, Israel was not able to stand against their enemies. "Therefore the children of Israel could not stand before their enemies, but turned their backs before their enemies because they were accursed: neither will I be with you anymore, except ye destroy the accursed from among you" (Joshua 7:12). For Israel to even get back into the game to win, they had to get rid of the sin in the camp. When Joshua confronted Achan, he confessed, "When I saw among the spoils a goodly Babylonish garment, and two hundred shekels of silver, and a wedge of gold of fifty shekels weight, then I coveted them, and took them; and, behold, they are hid in the earth in the midst of my tent, and the silver under it" (Joshua 7:21). God told Joshua to "get the sin from among you."

Obedience is to obey God, no matter the cost. If Joshua expected to win any more battles against his enemies, he had to get rid of the sin in his camp. Joshua understood that to believe God is to obey God. True faith is obedience. He found the sin in the camp and dealt with it. It is possible that hidden sin in our lives can hinder victories. I believe Joshua would have dealt with the sin before he fought with Ai, but it was hidden from him. His defeat was a wake-up call to pray, and when he prayed,

God revealed the hidden thing that displeased him. If you are defeated in an area where you know that you should be winning, go to the Lord in prayer, and He will reveal it to you. But once God reveals the problem, take action and stone it.

Stoning means to kill it. Anything that is displeasing God, kill it out of your life. Paul said, "I die daily" (1 Corinthians 15:31). Your own will can be displeasing to God if your will is not his will for your life. "I beseech you therefore, brethren, by the mercies of God, that ye present your bodies a living sacrifice, holy, acceptable unto God, which is your reasonable service" (Romans 12:1). "Present your body as a living sacrifice" means that you are willing to kill your own will and desire for God's will. Jesus was obedient unto death and calls for believers to commit their lives totally to his will. "And he said to them all, if any man will come after me, let him deny himself, and take up his cross daily, and follow me. For whosoever will save his life shall lose it: but whosoever will lose his life for my sake, the same shall save it" (Luke 9:23-24).

Joshua had to find the sin, stone it, and then burn it. Fire destroys but yet purifies. When something is burned to ashes, it is no longer useful in its original intent. Its former use is no longer. Through the fire of the Holy Ghost, we can be purified from unrighteous and old sinful desires (Mathew 3:11). "If we confess our sins, he is faithful and just to forgive us our sins, and to cleanse us from all unrighteousness" (1 John 1:9). God does not just want to forgive us of our sins, but He wants to cleanse us all unrighteousness. God desires that we be holy. "As obedient children, not fashioning yourselves according to the former lusts in your ignorance: But as he which hath called you is holy, so be ye holy in all manner of conversation;

Because it is written, Be ye holy; for I am holy" (1 Peter 1:14-16).

A life aligned with God's will is a life that is pleasing to God, and when a person's ways please the Lord, He will make His enemies be at peace with Him (Proverbs 16:7). Refuse to allow habitual sin to hinder the amazing things that God wants to do in your life. No matter how difficult it may be, stay in the will of God and pursue destiny against the odds.

CHAPTER 7
REMATCH

Never make failure final, especially when you believe with all your heart that God gave you the desire to complete a specific goal. Most times, when we fail to achieve a thing, it because of a lack of preparation or information. Preparation is a proceeding, measure, or provision by which one prepares for something. Preparation is being ready for the task you wish to accomplish. Many opportunities are missed because of a lack of preparation.

I remember as a teenager, I took a friend with me on a job interview. My dad got me the job through a friend, so pretty much the job was mine but, in my immaturity, instead of going alone, I brought one of my best friends at the time. Needless to say, my friend got the job and not me.

The job was being a caretaker of an apartment building with mopping, cleaning, and some handyman work. When the manager, who was a maintenance man looking for a helper, interviewed us, my friend did more talking than I did, and he was more familiar with certain tools and communicated more effectively than I did with the gentleman. As a result, my friend was hired instead of me, and it was my interview.

Even though it was my interview, my friend was more prepared than I was. He was not even looking for a job but took the job that was set up for me to have. Of course, I should have never brought him to my interview, but I never thought he would get the job. He kept that job for many years, too. It was my opportunity, but my friend's experience got him the job over me. He was prepared by his experience; I was not. I was the one that had the connection, but my lack of preparation and skill forfeited me the opportunity. My dad could get me the interview, but I was not prepared for the job.

Unlike my dad, God would rather that we be prepared for the opportunities that He has for us. Prep time is imperative to fulfill any task of significance. Esther, in the Book of Esther, had to go through a time of preparation before she could be the queen. There was a time of preparation between David being anointed to be king and him actually being enthroned as king. It took thirty years for Jesus to enter his public ministry that only lasted three years. Samuel, the prophet, had years with Eli, the prophet, before he became Israel's prophet. Prep time is the time you focus on sharpening your skills.

Study, meditate, and dream. Study for knowledge and understanding. Psalm 1 is clear that mediation on God's Word helps you to see and understand. "But his delight is in the law of the Lord; and in his law doth he meditate day and night. And he shall be like a tree planted by the rivers of water, that bringeth forth his fruit in his season; his leaf also shall not wither; and whatsoever he doeth shall prosper" (Psalms 1:2-3).

Meditating day and night is studying, seeking clarity, and understanding. What can make studying easy is loving to learn, loving wisdom, and loving the results of what you have learned.

The Bible says that when you meditate on the law of day and night that you will be like a tree planted by the rivers of water. A tree that is planted grows. God is saying when you meditate on His Word, you grow. Learning the right things results in growth. It is impossible to grow mentally and spiritually with learning and studying. Not only are you planted, but you are planted by the rivers of waters. Meaning that learning, studying, and meditating on God's Word is feeding you and sustaining you.

Then the Word says that you will bring forth fruit in your season. Fruit is a result of the knowledge you've gain. When you know better, you can do better. When you know more, you can do more. His leaf also shall not wither. You learning and increasing in wisdom is not in vain. And the last part of verse three is my favorite it says, and whatsoever he does shall prosper. Information and knowledge of the Word of God increases the possibilities of you prospering in whatever you do for the Lord.

Now, if that can work for the Word of God, I believe that we can use that same method to study to be a neurosurgeon. Meditating and studying a desired subject increases your chances of prospering in that area of choice. I believe that God called us to succeed in every area of life. "Beloved, I wish above all things that thou mayest prosper and be in health, even as thy soul prospereth" (3 John 1:2). Everything that a Christian makes up his or her mind to do is absolutely possible if we believe, study, and meditate on what we are trying to accomplish nothing is impossible.

In Joshua 7, Joshua lost the battle in Ai, a battle that he should have, without a doubt, won. He lost because of what he did not know. Achan had put what was consecrated to God in his own tent (Joshua 7:20-21). That insurrection kindled God's anger, and Joshua went into battle without God's blessing. God's blessing was the key ingredient to Israel's victories. When we fail, it is usually because we failed to do what it takes to win every time. Joshua did not check his camp before he went into battle.

When I used to be an emergency medical technician, before we drove the ambulance out of the garage to start our shift, we had to examine the ambulance to make sure that it was fully stocked with all of the emergency supplies that we would need. We also had to check the ambulance itself to make sure that the tires, oil, antifreeze, etc., were good; the ambulance needed to be fit for the road. We did not want to break down with a patient on board.

If Joshua would have followed up and examined his camp to make sure that everyone had followed God's instructions, he would have fixed the problem and would have been prepared for the battle. Or Joshua could have even prayed first before going into the battle at Ai. He prayed after they were defeated, not before. If he would have prayed before the battle, God would have said there is sin in the camp.

Being fully prepared for every task is essential to being successful. The good thing is that you can learn from your failures. Most fail many times before they succeed. There are wise lessons in failure if you take heed to them. Once you learn where your mistakes are, you can fix them and start over again. Joshua fixed that problem in his camp with Achan and had a rematch with the men of Ai and defeated them. Whatever you were unsuccessful in, if it really means that much to you to obtain it, try going for it again. Prepare yourself by training and getting all the information you need to succeed and go after it again.

Rematch means doing it a second time. Some of us may need more than two rematches, but the key is to keep fighting until you win. If it means that you must keep learning, then keep learning. Keep training your mind, body, and soul until you get the victory. If it takes a rematch for you to win, go for it. Go for it until it is hard for you to fail. Pursue destiny against the odds.

CHAPTER 8
LEGACY MINDED

Legacy - *a gift of property, especially personal property, as money, by will; a bequest.*

The other day, while enjoying the presence of my three-month-old grandson, I was filled with joy at the thought of starting an investment financial account for him. *By the time he is twenty-five years old, he will have a decent nest egg.* The idea of that for me is to give my grandson a head start in life. I think that the true testimony of success is when your children's children can benefit from it. "A good man leaveth an inheritance to his children's children: and the wealth of the sinner is laid up for the just" (Proverbs 13:22).

A good parent is mindful to leave an inheritance for their grandchildren. What you were not able to do for your children should be done for your grandchildren. I know in my case when Cynthia and I got married, we were working hard to feed our small family. We could not do what we wanted to do for our children at the beginning of marriage because we were working hard just to keep everything together.

When you are young and starting a family, it can be incredibly challenging, but through faith and determination, we made it. I learned from many mistakes that I have made with my own family that now my grandchildren can benefit from. Partly growing up, I did not have financial literacy, which is a major key if you are going to leave an inheritance for your children and grandchildren. Because I have learned some financial secrets and now doing better than I was before now, I can be a blessing to my grandson's financial future.

I do not remember meeting my grandmother on my mother's side of the family. She died before I was of age to know her as grandma. But my grandmother's sister took the place in my life that my grandmother was not able to fulfill. Even though she was my grand-aunt, she was like a grandmother to me and my siblings. Her name was Jessie Mae Sivills. She was an intricate part of my life, and the memory of her still inspires me to this very day.

Jessie Mae Sivills, affectionately known as Aunt Jessie, was a hard worker. She understood the importance of saving a dollar. She taught me that if you get a quarter, save a nickel. As a single black woman, she was highly successful. She had a good job, and she owned a beautiful co-op apartment that came with a doorman and swimming pool. That was very impressive, especially back in those days.

She was also a seamstress. She made her own clothes. She made an outfit or two for me back in the day. One day I used an Izod logo off a shirt that someone gave me that I could not fit. I took the shirt to Aunt Jessie with a jacket that I thought was a nice jacket and asked her to sow the alligator on the left front pocket of the jacket. She took the tag from inside the Izod shirt and remove the tag from inside my jacket and replace it with the Izod tag that was in the shirt. It made the jacket look like an authentic Izod jacket.

The kids in school loved my jacket and asked me where I purchased it. I told them Macy's. I know I lied. Please do not hold it against me. I was about twelve years old then. But I looked good and did not have to pay Izod prices, which was too costly for us to purchase back then.

Aunt Jessie knew how to save money. If we needed any financial help, Aunt Jessie would be the person to help us. I remember one day I asked her for some money to buy a new goose down coat from Macy's department store. Her reply was, "How much do you have for the coat?" I had nothing. Aunt Jessie was teaching me a valuable lesson as a young child. The lesson was that if I wanted anything that I should do my absolute best to work towards that goal on my own before asking anyone for help.

The principle here is that you cannot expect people to do for you what you are not willing to do for yourself. Aunt Jessie still purchased the coat for me, but I never forgot the lesson. When it was time for me and my siblings to go to college, my Aunt Jessie had saved up money for each of us to go to college. It was four of us. That was a tremendous blessing and load off my mom and dad. Aunt Jessie prepared for us an inheritance. Now I did not go to college at the time, but Aunt Jessie gave me the money at a time when I desperately needed it, and it blessed me and my wife in our newlywed days.

God promised to give Abraham land that he would leave as

an inheritance to his seed, who became a nation. The children of Israel are the seed of Abraham. "Now the Lord had said unto Abram, Get thee out of thy country, and from thy kindred, and from thy father's house, unto a land that I will shew thee: And I will make of thee a great nation, and I will bless thee, and make thy name great; and thou shalt be a blessing: And I will bless them that bless thee, and curse him that curseth thee: and in thee shall all families of the earth be blessed. So, Abram departed, as the Lord had spoken unto him; and Lot went with him: and Abram was seventy and five years old when he departed out of Haran. And Abram took Sarai his wife, and Lot his brother's son, and all their substance that they had gathered, and the souls that they had gotten in Haran; and they went forth to go into the land of Canaan; and into the land of Canaan they came. And Abram passed through the land unto the place of Shechem, unto the plain of Moreh. And the Canaanite was then in the land. And the Lord appeared unto Abram, and said, Unto thy seed will I give this land: and there built he an altar unto the Lord, who appeared unto him" (Genesis 12:1-7).

The land that God gave Abraham was also promised to his children's children. Actually, the land was for Abraham's bloodline. When God blesses you, He blesses you with your bloodline in mind. The blessing is never just for you; it is for your children, grandchildren, and their grandchildren, and it becomes a never-ending cycle of blessings for your bloodline. When we are legacy minded, we are working with others in mind instead of just ourselves. Givers think of others, not just themselves. Work with the bigger picture in mind, and that's legacy. When your work outlives you, that's legacy. Work with the mindset of leaving something behind. You will be loved and appreciated for generations. Abraham is known for being the father of many nations. His work, sacrifice, and obedience unto God became a legacy that not only his bloodline benefited from, but from those that joined His family through marriage. Even those that converted to his faith. "And if ye be Christ's, then are ye Abraham's seed, and heirs according to the promise" (Galatians 3:29). Jesus Christ is of the bloodline of Abraham, and because of the promise that God made Abraham, if we are believers in Jesus Christ, we become adopted into Abraham's family and inherit the same promises that God promised Abraham and his seed. Now Abraham is honored and credited for his sacrifice by many nations because of his thoughtfulness to leave a legacy. Pursue destiny against the odds and secure a legacy for your children's children.

CHAPTER 9
PUT YOUR FOOT ON ITS NECK

"And it came to pass, when they brought out those kings unto Joshua, that Joshua called for all the men of Israel, and said unto the captains of the men of war which went with him, Come near, put your feet upon the necks of these kings. And they came near and put their feet upon the necks of them" (Joshua 10:24).

As Joshua possessed the land of Canaan, there were five kings that were not willing to give up their cities. But if God gives you the land, whoever is in it is occupying it illegally. I believe that there are things that are yours by God's doing, but the forces of darkness refuse to let it go. Just as the prince of Persia (fallen angel) in Daniel's day influence the mind of Nebuchadnezzar. There are seducing spirits that are not God governing leaders of countries, states, and cities. Remember that the devil is the prince of the power of the air working in the children of disobedience (Ephesians 2:2).

These five kings refuse to give in to Joshua and the children of Israel even though they knew that God was with Joshua. Everyone in Canaan heard how God brought Israel out of Egypt with a mighty hand. Joshua had already conquered Jericho, Ai and Gideon submitted. Yet, these five kings wanted to war against Joshua and the children of Israel. The enemy knows that the blessing is yours, yet he still fights against you. The devil knows that God said that you are healed by Jesus stripes. Yet he fights against your health.

The prosperity is yours, and the devil knows it, yet he fights you for it. He wants to keep you from getting all that God has for you. Do not let the devil keep your stuff. Fight the good fight of faith. (1 Timothy 6:12) The devil is your adversary, the prince, and the power of the air. Air represents spirit because it is not seen, only felt or revealed by other things it affects. Like you cannot see the wind, but you know that the wind exists by the leaf it blows down the street or by the balloon or kite gliding in the sky. Just like the mind is considered spirit because it cannot be read by an X-ray or MRI. And the devil has access to the mind. That is why we need the mind of Christ, which is the Word of God (Philippians 2:5).

Fear is a spirit. "For God hath not given us the spirit of fear; but of power, and of love, and of a sound mind" (2 Timothy 1:7).

Faith is a spirit. "We having the same spirit of faith, according to as it is written, I believed, and therefore have I spoken; we also believe, and therefore speak;" (2 Corinthians 4:13).And faith comes by hearing the Word of God (Romans 10:17). And the Word of God is the Sword of the Spirit. The Word is what you use to fight against all the oppositions in your life.

Joshua and the children of Israel stood on the Word of God and were determined to fight against the five kings and their armies. As they were at war, God began to fight for Israel and sent a hailstorm on their enemies. God killed more people in a hailstorm than Joshua and Israel did by the sword. When you believe God and pursue in faith to possess the promises of the Lord, God will fight you with you. God will always fight with you when you believe.

After seeing their man slaughtered by a hailstorm and the sword of Joshua, the five kings ran and hid in a cave. It was told to Joshua that the kings hid in a cave. Joshua instructed his men to seal the kings in the cave until he was finished slaughtering their men. When Joshua had won the battle, he went to the cave where the five were sealed and told his men to bring the five kings out of the cave. Joshua told the captains of his army to put their feet on their necks.

Putting their feet on their enemy's necks represented that these kings were under subjection. It displayed power and authority. Sometimes you must let the enemy know that you have the power. "And he said unto them, I beheld Satan as lightning fall from heaven. Behold, I give unto you power to tread on serpents and scorpions, and over all the power of the enemy: and nothing shall by any means hurt you" (Luke 10:18-19).

If you are a born-again Christian, God has given you power over the devil. God has given you power through his son Jesus Christ. No witch, warlock, or any other creature can stop you. You have the power and anointing of Christ Jesus on your life, and in the name of Jesus, every knee has got to bow, and every tongue must confess that Jesus is Lord.

Lord means ruler, and Jesus is ruler over the devil, and Jesus has given you the authority to rule over the devil. Therefore, the devil is subject to you in Jesus's name. So put your foot on his neck and let him know whose boss. Go and possess the land of promise. You might have to fight for it through prayer, faith, and hard work but know that you have the power to overcome any opposition that comes your way in Jesus's name.

Put your foot on the neck of the spirit of poverty, sickness, disease, divorce, generational curses, and oppression by taking authority according to the Word of God in Jesus's name. Decree increase in your business, peace in your home, and joy in your heart. Live life like you are a winner. Jesus has given you the power.

Joshua and his men put their feet on the necks of kings. Kings rule kingdoms. Kings have dominion and power. The only reason that the kings' armies fought Joshua and the children of Israel is because they were commanded by their kings to do so. Once the king is dead, his followers will scatter without direction. Satan is the king of the kingdom of darkness, but Jesus is the King of Kings, and he has given every believer authority over Satan. "Submit yourselves therefore to God. Resist the devil, and he will flee from you" (James 4:7).

Once you operate in the authority that Jesus has given you, the devil and all his cohorts must flee because even demons reverence the power of Jesus Christ. "Thou believest that there is one God; thou doest well: the devils also believe, and tremble" (James 2:19). So, live your life with your foot on the neck of any demonic force or power that hinders you from living the life that God has promised you in His Holy Word. You have the authority and power to pursue destiny against the odds.

CHAPTER 10
A WINNER'S HEART

"But the Lord said unto Samuel, Look not on his countenance, or on the height of his stature; because I have refused him: for the Lord seeth not as man seeth; for man looketh on the outward appearance, but the Lord looketh on the heart" (1 Samuel 16:7).

To have heart is to never lose tenacity, strength, or faith regardless of the circumstances. To have heart is to be courageous. To have heart causes you at times to be a maverick to dare to do what others would never do even if you have to it alone. When the prophet Samuel was instructed by God to anoint the next king of Israel because God rejected King Saul, he sent him to the house of Jesse.

Jesse had sons that looked the part, and Samuel was impressed by their countenance and height, but God had refused them. But Jesse's son, David, who was not even considered to be king, was the one who God chose. Man looks on the outward appearance, but God looks at the heart. God chose

David to be king because he knew his heart. It is a wonderful thing to know that God sees the heart.

The disposition of a person's heart is who they really are. "For as he thinketh in his heart, so is he..." (Proverbs 23:7). Therefore, the meditation of your heart is vital. It describes to God everything about you. "Let the words of my mouth, and the meditation of my heart, be acceptable in thy sight, O Lord, my strength, and my redeemer" (Psalms 19:14). The meditation of your heart should be kept pure because God sees the heart. A faithful heart is acceptable unto God.

Jesus said, "Ye have heard that it was said by them of old time, Thou shalt not commit adultery: But I say unto you, That whosoever looketh on a woman to lust after her hath committed adultery with her already in his heart" (Matthew 5:27-28). Even if a person has not actually committed adultery, because it is done in that person's imagination or heart, God says it has already been done. Because as a man thinks in his heart, so is he (Matthew 12:34). "Keep thy heart with all diligence; for out of it are the issues of life" (Proverbs 4:23).

Your heart is the total essence of who you are. I know that we like to dress up the outside, but the truth is, inside your heart is the real you. Out of your heart flows the issues of life. Most issues in a person's life are a complete reflection of their heart's attitude. So even though people cannot see your heart, God can. And He responds to the heart of that person, not the mouth of that person. Jesus said, "These people draweth nigh unto me with their mouth, and honoureth me with their lips; but their heart is far from me" (Matthew 15:8). That is amazing to me. You cannot fool God with your words because God reads your heart. So, if the heart cannot be kept secret from

God, then the heart needs to be pure before God to be accepted by God. "God blesses those whose hearts are pure, for they will see God" (Matthew 5:8). People can misjudge people, but God can never misjudge because he reads the heart of people. God knows who is in faith or not. It is with the heart that man believes (Romans 10:10).

A winner's heart is a heart of faith. A heart that trusts in the Lord. David loved God, and God knew it because God knew David's heart. David stood up to the giant Goliath when he was only a young boy. But God knew that David would stand up and fight for the children of Israel before David's father, Jesse, knew of King Saul because God knew David's heart.

Joshua was a slave who became a warrior. He believed God had given the children of Israel the land of Canaan. Joshua entered the Promised Land while those who came out of Egypt with him died in the wilderness except for Caleb. Joshua believed. A winner's heart is a believing heart. It is a heart that is pure and positive. It is a heart that is guarded against doubt and fear. A winner's heart is a brave heart.

Not only did Joshua enter the Promised Land by faith, but he overcame his enemies that were in the Promised Land. There are enemies where your promise is, but you can overcome them. Joshua fought until he defeated all his enemies. He was not afraid because he trusted that God was with him. Joshua occupied the Promised Land. He entered, overcame, and occupied.

Pursue the promise until you enter that promise. Then overcome all the obstacles and oppositions that are in the Promised Land. Then occupy, live, and take up residence in your Promise

Land. Know that where there is no wealth, there will be little struggle, but where the wealth is, there will be many struggles.

The land of promise flows with milk and honey. It is a wealthy place so expect warfare to obtain it because of your enemies that are there. Know that anything that is worth having does not come easy. You will have to fight the good fight of faith to occupy your Promised Land but know that God shall fight with you. Joshua died at rest in the Promised Land. We are all going to die unless we are living in the time when Jesus returns, and the believers are raptured. But if that is not the case, you are going to die. So, die living in your promise and not in the process.

A winner's heart comes out of Egypt, which represents bondage, makes it through the wilderness, which represents the process, and enters Canaan land, which represents the promise. Live the promise that God gave you. Be determined not to die in the process. It will get hard at times but know that God is with you to fulfill that promise.

Pursue destiny against the odds.

PART II
HER PERSPECTIVE
By Dr. Cynthia McInnis

CHAPTER 11
A GOOD REPORT

"And Caleb stilled the people before Moses, and said, let us go up at once, and possess it; for we are well able to overcome it"

— *NUMBERS 13:30*

So, check it! After years and years of bondage and *not enough* in Egypt, followed by a long season of *just enough* in the wilderness, God's people are finally ready for a season of *more than enough.* God told Moses to send men to search the land of Canaan and assured them that it was already theirs by saying, "which I give unto the children of Israel." Isn't it funny how challenges often make us hear *in part*? Giants, monsters, threats, and challenges manage to give us selective hearing when it comes to what God has already said. For some of us, this would have been a no-brainer! God said it's mine, so ... duhhhhhh, it's mine.

God was so serious about His Word that He told Moses to

choose a leader from every tribe to search the land that was already theirs. He never said to assess the land to see if you could inhabit it because He already knew they would; after all, it was already theirs. Moses told them to "see the land what it is; and the people that dwelleth therein, whether they be strong or weak, few or many, and whether the land is that they dwell in, whether it be good or bad; and what cities they be that they dwell in, whether in tents, or in strongholds; and what the land is, whether it be fat or lean, whether there be wood therein, or not;" That is to say, make assessments, not conclusions or determinations.

I have run daycare centers for the past 14 years and studied Early Childhood Education for an equal number of years. While many things have changed over the years, one thing remains constant, and that is the rules for *observations and assessments*. All childcare professionals are taught to observe but not to conclude. The observations simply say what the observer sees at daily, weekly, or monthly intervals. For example, the four-year-old boy threw the toy truck in the direction of the girls repeatedly. He cannot say the four-year-old boy hates girls and was angry at them, so he kept throwing the truck in their direction. That is not an observation but a drawn conclusion and, very possibly, a failed assessment. The assessment *includes* the observation and helps the teacher to prepare for any challenges that may be presented by the observations.

This is what was supposed to have happened when the leaders returned to Moses with their report. Moses already knew there would be possible challenges, but he did not cancel the assignment. Instead, he said, "And be ye of good courage, and bring of the fruit of the land." Perhaps they needed this to keep them on their A-game. Perhaps the children of Israel, who were awaiting their return, would be further encouraged by seeing and tasting the fruit of the land. Surely it had to taste better than that manna!

The brook, Eshcol, produced great clusters of grapes, juicy pomegranates, and sweet figs! I would certainly think that this was all they would need to satisfy their uncertainties! But, as they returned from the forty-day journey, their thoughts were divided, and the fruit was simply not enough to convince them all.

When Moses and the children of Israel saw them returning with the fruit of the land, Moses prepared himself for their report. The report went like this; *Well, Moses, we came to the land that you sent us to, and just like you said, surely it did flow with milk and honey, and this is the fruit we found there.* So far, so good, right? Nope! This part was followed by a, *nevertheless*! "The people are strong; the cities are walled and very great; and we saw the children of Anak there too! The Amalekites, Hittites, Jebusites, and Amorites dwell in the mountains, and then there's the Canaanites who dwell by the sea..."

It was that *nevertheless* that disturbed Caleb, who was one of the eldest of the leaders and clearly had had enough of their negative observations. I would venture to say that their story was beginning to cause unrest among the people. I can just hear them saying, "Oooh, oh my, Oh Lord," after hearing about all of those *ites* in the land! Caleb quieted the people. And made this very bold and overt suggestion. "Let us go up at once and possess it; for we are well able to overcome it!"

Now, here is where their observation and assessment turned into a conclusion. "But the men that went up with him said, we be not able to go up against the people; for they are stronger than we." What? *Not able? They are stronger than we?* I can imagine that Caleb's blood began to boil! They continued their *evil* report with such terms as, "it is a land that eateth up its inhabitants thereof, and all the people that we saw in it are men of great stature." Hold on here! Wait a minute? Would God give you a land that *eats up* its inhabitants? If the land is eating up the inhabitants, how did the people become men of *great stature?*

Their final, expressed conclusion revealed the problem with their entire report. "And there we saw the giants, the sons of Anak, which come of the giants; and we were in our own sight as grasshoppers, and so we were in their sight."

First, they saw the giants. Giants are very easy to see. It is very difficult to hide a giant. In fact, the very strength of the giant is not his arm but his presence. Giants are extremely intimidating and most often never even have to fight. Once people see them, they often retreat in fear. If they saw the giants, surely Caleb saw them too. Not to mention, God saw the giants long before the men of Israel ever got there. The difference here is perception; They saw the giants as intimidating threats, but Caleb and Joshua saw them as a challenge! They understood that in order to get the grapes, they had to defeat those giants, and all the odds were stacked against them. They had to pursue against the odds, and the question became, how bad do you want those grapes?

Caleb and Joshua understood that although there may have been more of them in Canaan than there were with Israel in the wilderness, they were still able to defeat them because they had the champion on their side. Our great defender! Our strong tower! He would never be defeated. It was God that promised them the land and reassured them that it was already theirs but not without a challenge.

How many times have we wanted the prize but ran from the challenge? How many times did we work our way out of our promise by trying desperately to avoid challenges? Challenges are made to be met, not avoided, and you need a *Caleb perception* to get that done. You've heard it before. At some point, we must stop telling our God about the problem and start telling the problem about our God. We must bring our very real observations to the assessment stages and strategize to meet every possible challenge that comes with those observations. Once the observations have been matched with the assessments, we will be ready to come back from it with a good report! "...let us go up at once and possess it; for we are well able to overcome it."

CHAPTER 12
GOD'S TIMING

Well, if you read the Bible like I read it, you are sitting on the edge of your seat, waiting for Moses to make a decision. Would he join in the fervor and faith of Joshua and Caleb's good report, or would he indulge the fear provoked by those who brought the evil report? This is clearly the time for possession of the promise, but it is met with great challenges. I would venture to say that *whenever* it is time to possess the promises of God, challenges appear.

The silence is broken in Numbers 14, with the shrill of those voices who were affected by the evil report. "And all the congregation lifted up their voice and cried; and the people wept that night." It was as if they heard nothing that Caleb said, only the evil report. It was as if their feet had never touched dry ground at the bottom of the Red Sea! If God could open the sea and swallow up their enemies, why would they be so totally dismantled by the evil report?

There is something about painful experiences that dull the mind and cause hearts to faint in the presence of yet another painful experience. God eventually delivered them, but it took Him some four hundred years. Talk about God's timing! How do we handle situations that seem to take God a long, long time to intervene? Surely, none of us has had a personal dilemma that lasted 400 years, but when we talk about systemic racism, the injustice of slavery, or the Holocaust, we might get a better idea of what the children of Israel were feeling at the time.

The evil report brought them back to a long history of pain and horrific memories. They were finally free. They had been through the wilderness, surviving with just enough, but at least they didn't have to fight any giants! Misunderstanding God's timing can make you comfortable in the wilderness. Although the wilderness was sufficient, it paled in comparison to The Promised Land. If we do not keep our hearts and minds on the promise, we can become complacent with not enough or just okay. It appeared that Israel had let time become the enemy of their faith!

Fear is usually accompanied by its two cousins; murmuring and accusation. Whenever people are afraid, they need to find someone to blame, and, in most cases, it is the leader. "And all the children of Israel murmured against Moses and against Aaron: and the whole congregation said unto them, Would God that we had died in the land of Egypt! or would God we had died in this wilderness! And wherefore hath the LORD brought us unto this land, to fall by the sword, that our wives and our children should be a prey? were it not better for us to return into Egypt?" And they said one to another, let us make a captain, and let us return into Egypt."

Here, we can easily conclude that this attitude, although it is understood based on the circumstances, is a potential reason for the long wait. While it is easy to blame God and/or questionable leadership for delays in the fulfillment of God's promises, we must also consider that our responses to challenges may be potential causes for those delays. We learn later that this was exactly the case. Their poor response to the challenge cost them one additional year in the wilderness for each day the spies spent in Canaan! They were ready to "make a captain" and return to Egypt! Make a captain? Were they really serious? Fear, frustration, anger, and even disappointment are never valid excuses for breaching spiritual protocol. You can't just *make a captain!*

I am certain that the thought may have crossed Caleb's mind; if not for him, surely for Joshua, who was already known as Moses's number-two man. However, in order for Joshua to become the new leader, there would have to be a transition of power according to spiritual protocol. In essence, Joshua could not make a move without the current leader, Moses'. Although the situation was dire, and the land was ready, it was simply not his time.

"Now after the death of Moses the servant of the Lord it came to pass, that the Lord spake unto Joshua the son of Nun, Moses's minister ..." At the time of this book's writing, we happen to be in the midst of a very controversial and unprecedented transition of power. The man who once served as the number-two man has been elected to become the number-one man.

The Democratic former Vice President of the United States has just been determined to be the winner of the 2020 election.

It is this transition of power that has caused so much political unrest that the very nation feels dangerously divided. While some revel in the celebration of the far-left victory, others cry "scandal" from the far right. One part of our country appears to appeal to a more democratic socialistic, almost Godless, standpoint while the other seeks to restore the values that America once stood for as in the adage, *in God we trust,* even if it is chanted from beneath white-robed and hooded faces. The incumbent has yet to concede and congratulate the newly elected official. In plain English, it's a hot stinking mess!

While the world is fighting this out, let us gauge our focus on this biblical transition of power. While Moses led the children of Israel from Egypt to and through the wilderness, Joshua remained, *his minister.* While there remain a plethora of descriptions for the term minister, I prefer to stick with the one most widely accepted, his *servant.* Joshua was Moses's number-two man! It appears here that even when God spoke to Joshua before this time, it was insignificant, at least not significant enough for a biblical mention. But Chapter 1 begins specifically with God's words to Joshua… but only *after the death of Moses.*

While we may all be able to hear the voice of God speaking to us, leaders hear from God to *lead.* As Moses's number-two man, Joshua did not have to learn to hear from God, but he did have to learn how to follow God's instructions for leadership. This began explicitly with holding on to his vision while serving another's. Not only did Joshua get to see Moses in startling victory, but he also got to see Moses fail, be afraid, be uncertain, be angry, and be completely wrong; while at the same time, remain in position as the servant-leader to the children of Israel.

Now that Moses was dead, Joshua had become his appointed successor (Deuteronomy 31). While this appeared to be a great honor, Joshua had already been warned by Moses that God said the children of Israel would continue to be a stiff-necked people who would rebel from the ways of the Lord. Whatever God would say next would most certainly be met with a challenge. First off, while Joshua was a great student-servant of Moses, he was not, in fact, Moses. God used Moses for the generation of Israel that needed Moses and would use Joshua to develop an entirely different generation. Joshua would have to pursue his assignment against the odds. The Joshua-led generation would do things differently than the Moses-led generation, and those who were young and zealous and could not appreciate the years that Joshua had spent with Moses would ultimately be difficult to lead.

Joshua's challenge began when he returned from Canaan with the other leaders. Joshua and Caleb had a vision and believed whole-heartedly that they were well able to conquer the land and possess it, but Joshua could not make a move without Moses'. This display of spiritual protocol is one that is worth mentioning. Although Joshua and Caleb were zealous and ready to move forward, the final say had to come from the current leader.

It is in situations like these that we have seen an unfortunate breach in spiritual protocol over the years. Respect for leadership has dwindled in such a way that open rebellion has become blatant. Public slandering and ridicule of leadership continue on social media platforms where people hide behind digital screens and spew out whatever opinions they feel each day. Media bias that targets religion one week and politics the next adds to the infectious trend of leadership-bashing. Fact-checking is pretty much non-existent. *"I know it's true because it was on the news"* mentalities tend to govern our day.

Joshua understood that any rebellion against the current leader would be repeated in the life of the successor, so while it may have been burning him up inside that Moses did not immediately move on the good report of Caleb, Joshua did not make a move before his time. This will prove to be a sterling quality that leads to ultimate victories for the children of Israel.

CHAPTER 13
BREAKING FREE: FROM A SLAVE TO A WARRIOR

J oshua, son of Nun, was from the tribe of Ephraim. He was a slave in Egypt and fled with Moses and the children of Israel during the great Exodus. It is said that he was such a faithful servant that *"he never moved from the tent of Moses."* His name was originally Hoshea (Hosea) but was changed by Moses to Yehoshua (Joshua). Right before he would leave to spy the land of Canaan, Moses, fearing the spies would fail, added the letter "yud" to Hoshea's name, changing it to Yehoshua, which means "May God save you."

There is no previous mention of Joshua being a warrior until the Amalekites attacked Moses and the children of Israel in Rephidim. It was only at the command of Moses that Joshua would fight the Amalekites. "And Moses said unto Joshua, choose us out men, and go out, fight with Amelek ... "So, Joshua **did as Moses had said to him, and fought with Amelek: ... and Joshua discomfited Amelek and his people with the edge**

of the sword." My point here is not that Joshua was a great warrior, although he certainly was, but that before that battle, Joshua was merely a slave and a servant. He became a warrior at the command of his leader.

As I read the Scripture, I saw no evidence of Joshua's resistance and no evidence of Joshua's history as a warrior; I only see the obedience of a true servant. It is after the battle with Amelek that Joshua became known as a fierce warrior. The Lord was with Joshua because he honored and served Moses. We cannot negate the fact that as long as Moses's hands were lifted, Israel remained victorious. A good servant always understands that their victories are directly related to the hands of those they serve. The God that was with Moses was also with Joshua.

We see another very interesting narrative during the battle at Rephidim. "But Moses's hands were heavy; and they took a stone, and put it under him, and he sat thereon; and Aaron and Hur stayed up his hands, the one on the one side, and the other on the other side, and his hands were steady until the going down of the sun."

I will share this biography of Aaron from "Who was Aaron in the Old Testament?" by Bibleask.com:

Aaron was a prophet, High priest, and the brother of Moses (Exodus 6:20; 15:20). While Moses grew up in the royal court, Aaron and his elder sister Miriam lived in Goshen. When Moses first confronted the Egyptian king about the Israelites, Aaron served as his brother's spokesman before Pharaoh (Exodus 4:10-17; 7:1). At the command of Moses, he let his rod turn into a snake (Exodus 7:10). Then he stretched out his rod in order to bring on the first three plagues (Exodus 8:6-19) to demonstrate to Pharaoh that they were sent from God. The Lord ordained that Aaron would have the priesthood for himself and his male descendants (Exodus 28:1). The rest of the tribe, the Levites, were given subordinate responsibilities within the sanctuary (Numbers 3).

At the battle with Amalek, Aaron was chosen with Hur to support the hands of Moses that held the "rod of God" (Exodus 17). When the revelation was given to Moses at Mount Sinai, his brother was the head of the elders who accompanied Moses on the way to the summit. Joshua went with Moses to the top, but Aaron and Hur remained behind (Exodus 32).

During the long absence of Moses on Mount Sinai, the people asked Aaron to make a Golden Calf as a visible image of the divinity, who had delivered them from Egypt (Exodus 32:1-6). Aaron yield to their demands. This incident brought God's destruction to the camp (Exodus 32:10; Exodus 32:25-35).

On one occasion, Miriam and her brother murmured about Moses's claim to be the LORD's prophet. But God affirmed Moses's office as the one with whom the LORD spoke face to face. Miriam was punished with leprosy for a brief period of time. Her brother pleaded with Moses to intercede for her, and Miriam was healed (Numbers 12).

A Levite named Korah led many to rebel against Moses's and his brother's claim to the priesthood (Numbers 16-17). But God punished the rebels, and they were destroyed (Numbers 16:25-35). And the Lord confirmed that Aaron alone should hold the high office by making his staff alone to blossom (Numbers 17:8).

Aaron, like Moses, was not permitted to enter Canaan because of the two brothers' impatience at Meribah (Numbers 20:12-13). Soon *after this incident, he with his son Eleazar and Moses ascended Mount Hor. There, Moses transferred the priestly garments from Aaron to Eleazar. Then, he died on the summit of the mountain, and the people mourned for him thirty days (Numbers 20:22-29).*

Aaron's life, apart from his shortcomings, was a clear demonstration of a man who served the Lord, devoted his life to the priesthood, and supported Moses as he led the nation of Israel from the Egyptian bondage to the promised land.

Neither Joshua nor Aaron and Hur were warriors before this time, but each of them played a very vital role in obtaining the victory for Israel during the battle with Amelek. They were Hebrew slaves who became warriors. It is important to know that warriors are not only those who fight with the sword, as was Joshua, but warriors are those who hold up the hands of the leader in the time of battle. Each role mattered.

Although Aaron had some personal challenges with Moses, he was still valuable. While Moses held up the rod, his symbol of faith, Aaron and Hur held up his hands when they got weary. They propped his arms upon a rock as he sat with his hands lifted, and Joshua was in the valley, slaying their enemies with the sword. Together they got the victory for Israel. "And the Lord said unto Moses, write this for a memorial in a book, and rehearse it in the ears of Joshua: for I will utterly put out the remembrance of Amelek from under heaven. And Moses built an altar, and called the name of it Jehovah, Nissi: for he said because the Lord hath sworn that the Lord will have war with Amelek from generation to generation."

We can go from mere slaves to sin, selfishness, and serenity to warriors in prayer, power, and praise. We can assess the battle, find our place, and help defeat every enemy that rises up against the body of Christ. Through spiritual warfare, observing spiritual protocol, and sincere obedience to leadership, there is no battle that is too great and no victory that cannot be attained.

CHAPTER 14
THE WILDERNESS

It is interesting to know that the children of Israel were getting prepared for the promised land while in the wilderness. I would think that it would make much more sense to train them in a land much like the land they were going into, but God chose a wilderness. "When they set out from Rephidim, they came to the wilderness of Sinai and camped in the wilderness; and there Israel camped in front of the mountain" (Exodus 19:1-2).

We must understand that once the children of Israel came out of a 400-year bondage in Egypt, they were a people with no, or at the very least, a conflicted identity. They had spent so much time in Egypt that their identity as God's chosen people had been intertwined with the mentality of the Hebrew slave. They needed to be re-established as a people before they were ready to occupy the land of promise.

I recall my husband and I applying for our first mortgage. While we knew the general idea was to borrow money from a bank to buy a house, we did not know the details. Our creditability needed to be established. We would have to be prepared to go from renters to homeowners. It was not enough to know that we were able to pay the loan, but our credit history would have had to be established. We would need a traceable history of established credit. After being denied the first time, our mindsets had to be re-established as potential homeowners. We would begin to be more conscious of our spending habits, timely bill payments, etc. This was no overnight sensation. It would take some time.

The children of Israel had many lessons to learn in the wilderness as they would be filled with doubt, fear, and general confusion. The promise of a land flowing with milk and honey sounds like a transition from bondage in Egypt to one of immediate gratification. A quick transition would have been a disaster for Israel. The land was already occupied by people who knew who they were. Israel would come in as a people without an identity and would have been slaughtered on the spot.

Many of the children of Israel had never known of the promise of God or simply lost faith in it by the time they were made free from Egypt. While they may have believed somewhat that they were indeed God's chosen people, it sure didn't feel like it after having been left in Egypt as slaves for so long. Many of them intermarried and adapted to the sinful ways of Egyptians. Their fear and reverence for God had to be established and re-established. This would happen in the wilderness.

My husband and I could have simply prayed to God to *give us the house* and waited for a miracle or learned the lessons required to establish the creditability required for using the bank's funding. We would learn that God's help was, in fact, helping us to learn what we needed to learn. As children of God, we have access to God's help, and knowing *how* He helps is tantamount to the time it takes for us to get what we are praying for. Also, knowing and following the requirements for obtaining help from God, just like knowing and following the requirements for obtaining a bank loan, will get it to us.

God knew that before the Israelites could occupy Canaan, they would have to have an identity. He would do this through a wilderness experience. There were no obvious resources in the wilderness. Even the major human necessities were lacking in the wilderness. There was water, but the water was bitter. The land was uncultivated, so there was no way to grow food or vegetation. It was in the wilderness that the Israelites would learn to completely depend on God for their help. Perhaps all that time in Egypt taught them systemic welfare; they would learn to eat what Pharaoh would provide or eat from the land that was not their own. This mentality would make them less God-dependent and more system-dependent. The wilderness would teach them to start again with nothing and to watch God provide.

God would provide for them but not without strict instructions. After singing and dancing in celebration of God's great providence, the Israelites traveled for three days by foot through the wilderness of Shur, finding no water. Finally, they came to some water, only to find it bitter and undrinkable! They named the place "Marah" or bitterness. While the *unfit-for-Canaan* people murmured against Moses, he cried out to God on their behalf. God gave Moses specific instructions to throw a tree into the bitter waters, and the water became sweet.

Lesson: God saw their need, heard the cry of their leader, and provided for them through his obedience. Instruction: " ... the waters were made sweet: there he made for them a statute and an ordinance, and there he proved them and said, if thou wilt diligently hearken to the voice of the Lord they God, and wilt do that which is right in his sight, and wilt give ear to his commandments, and keep all his statutes, I will put none of these diseases upon thee, which I have brought upon the Egyptians: for I am the Lord that health thee." It was not until after he had given them a lesson and an instruction that they came to Elim, where there were twelve wells of water and some seventy Palm trees.

It was not long after leaving the sweet waters of Elim that they came to the wilderness of Sin. Hungry and starving for food, once again, they murmured against Moses and reminded him of the welfare in Egypt. "... Would to God we had died by the hand of the Lord in Egypt, when we sat by the flesh pots and when we did eat bread to the full;..." (Exodus 16:3). Once again, God provided with specific instructions, " Then said the Lord unto Moses, Behold, I will rain bread from heaven for you; and the people shall go out and gather a certain rate every day, that I may prove them, whether they will walk in my law or no."

It is very obvious that God was establishing a relationship with His people while developing a very needed identity in them. It is no secret that God was using their wilderness experience to prepare them for his promise to them. It is also very important that they lived according to God's law in order to establish an identity *in* him. This is obviously very, very important to God and must be equally important to his people.

In our modern-day religious establishments, much of the focus is on the rules of religion and not the reality of a personal relationship with God. God is concerned with a relationship because this is what truly establishes identity. Knowing God personally is like having a personal relationship with a superpower who works for your team! When you are in a relationship with someone who is strong where you are weak, you can identify as strong. "And he said unto me, my grace is sufficient for thee: for my strength is made perfect in weakness …" (2 Corinthians 12:9).

The wilderness is a dry, uncultivated land with little or no resources. The inhabitants of the wilderness need to learn to depend on God by following his instructions. The children of Israel need to establish an identity as the children of God. They had come into the wilderness with a dry, uncultivated, resourceless identity that will require lesson upon lesson that can only be learned there.

CHAPTER 15
NO GAIN WITHOUT A FIGHT

It is interesting that moments before starting this chapter, I stopped to open the mail. In the mail, I found a Letter of Rejection from the zoning board regarding an upcoming community program we are preparing to start. As I shared the contents of the letter with my husband, both of us agreed that we are prepared to fight this rejection. I immediately called to request an appeal of their decision. Experience has taught us that there is no gain without a fight.

The children of Israel were entering into the promised land. Much of the generation that came out of Egypt had died in the wilderness; it simply took them too long to learn what they needed to learn. The nucleus of the new generation will follow Joshua into the unknown with faith and confidence. No more welfare. No more murmurings. No more uncertainty. "And they answered Joshua, saying, all that thou commandest us we will do, and whithersoever thou sendest us, we will go" (Joshua 1:16).

Not only were they prepared for war with the inhabitants of the land, but the voices in verse 16 were also prepared for any insurrection in the ranks. They were determined to possess the promised land. "Whosoever he be that doth rebel against thy commandment, and will not hearken unto thy words in all that thou commandest him, he shall be put to death: ..." There would be no tolerance for any consistent whining and murmurings of the rank. They had to be ready to fight.

First up was Jericho. This is where we learn that we only discover God's unseen help once we prepare to fight. Who knew that the inhabitants were already scared to death of the Israelites? Who knew they were shaking in their boots about the reputation of Israel's God? "And she said unto the men. I know that the Lord hath given you the land, and that your terror is fallen upon us, and that all the inhabitants of the land faint because of you. ... As soon as we heard of these things, our hearts did melt, neither did there remain any more courage in any man, because of you: for the Lord your God, he is God in heaven above, and in earth beneath."

Any warrior knows that, to the fearful, fear is a prerequisite for a losing battle and an asset to their opponent. Fear is something that is intangible! It is both an unseen liability and asset in battle. Joshua and the Israelites could not factor that in until they heard it from Rahab the Harlot.

Joshua and Caleb did not pray that their enemies disappear. They did not try to find a way around the conflict. They prepared to fight! The argument could have been made all day that God said the land was theirs, but the other nations had their own gods from whom they could say the same. This would not be a court case; it would be a battle. There are some things that are worth fighting for, and Canaan was one of them.

Fighting by faith is different from fighting in the flesh. Joshua and Caleb knew they were fighting for a promise that God made to them, and they knew their God to be infallible. When they got to Rahab's house, they learned that God was already working with and for them. They would have to fight, but the fight was fixed! The only way to lose the battle would be not to fight at all. There is no gain without a fight.

While we no longer engage in physical warfare as in Joshua's day, warfare is not a foreign term in Scripture. Philippians 2:25 and Philemon 1:2, Paul describes fellow Christians as "fellow soldiers." The image of a soldier is also used in 2 Timothy 2:3-4 as a metaphor for courage, loyalty, and dedication. Ephesians 6 discusses faith, righteousness, and other elements of Christianity as the armor of God.

The weapons of our warfare are no longer carnal but spiritual. We engage in spiritual warfare, and the same adage applies; there is no gain without a fight. We are admonished to resist the devil, and he will flee. Resistance symbolizes a spiritual push back. Christians who do not practice spiritual warfare are defeated Christians. Take note that the reputation that went before the Israelites was that their God would fight for them. If they had lost the battle for any reason, their enemies would conclude that their God had lost the battle for them; that he was unreliable or capable of failure. That is why it was necessary to have a leader who heard from God and would follow his instructions implicitly. Joshua had to follow God's instructions, even when they made no earthly sense. Marching around a wall for seven days, seven times a day, was ridiculous, but it worked.

When Christians either do not engage in spiritual warfare or cannot hear God's instructions, their defeat is reflected back to God. It is important that we win! We cannot be defeated, not just for our sakes but for the sake of the Kingdom. We must fight back by faith and trust God for the win. Whatever we desire is attainable by faith, but faith without works is dead being alone. Putting in work is fighting back by faith. When sickness infiltrates our bodies, changing our lifestyles, eating habits, and personal choices are called fighting back, putting in the work by faith. Some people get a diagnosis and immediately pray and/or ask for prayer. Of course, this is what we should do, but we must also make the necessary life changes that may contribute to disease reversal. I know it is common to simply continue eating what we eat and doing what we do and declare our healing by faith as if faith works like magic; One or two ala-ka-zams and whoosh!

Joshua knew that acquisition of Canaan was no magic trick. He was prepared to defeat his enemies by employing all of the skills he had developed in the wilderness. I've heard of mothers who run into burning buildings if their child is inside; some will do it for a pet. Is it wise? Probably not. Did they plan it? Absolutely not! But to them, the child or the pet is worth fighting for. Canaan was worth fighting for. Your peace is worth fighting for. Your marriage, your children, your sanity, your health, and your relationship with God is worth fighting for. Even If you die trying, death is swallowed up in victory, and either way, we win. Fight to win because there is no gain without a fight.

CHAPTER 16
FIND IT, STONE IT, BURN IT

Joshua 7-8

Next up, little ole Ai (pronounced Long A - YEE), a city with very few inhabitants and a very easy army to defeat. Joshua had been on a roll of conquests from the wilderness of Moab all the way to Syria, and the battle at Ai would be an easy win. Joshua sent a small company of warriors to Ai, expecting them to return with victory and all the spoils, as they did at Jericho. However, the smell of smoke and the gloomy feeling of unfamiliar defeat seriously changed the mood.

Joshua was completely taken aback by the news of Israel's defeat. He and his fellow defeated militia fell to their faces in grief. Joshua began a hysterical rant, much like those of the murmuring Israelites in the wilderness. "And Joshua said, "Alas, Sovereign Lord, why did you ever bring these people across the Jordan to deliver us into the hands of the Amorites to destroy us? If only we had been content to stay on the other side of the

Jordan! Pardon your servant, Lord. What can I say, now that Israel has been routed by its enemies? The Canaanites and the other people of the country will hear about this, and they will surround us and wipe out our name from the earth. What then will you do for your own great name?"

Can you imagine the other kneeling elders listening to their fearless leader whine like a baby in the face of unanticipated defeat? I get it. They had not lost a battle before, and they had a reputation for being undefeated. Oh, he carried on and laid it on thick! "The Canaanites and the other people in the country will hear about this, and they will surround us and wipe out our name from the earth." Really, Joshua? Had he forgotten who he was talking to? "What then will you do for your own great name?" Guess so.

Joshua was obviously devastated and afraid. We say some of the most *faithless* things when we are afraid. Joshua attributed Israel's loss to the military might of a small army. He babbled on and on about the Canaanites and the other inhabitants of their land, the same Canaanites and other *ites* they had seen when they spied out the land. It never occurred to him that God had this situation under control. Because of the defeat, Joshua misjudged his entire military history and the power of his God. Joshua was *having a moment.*

God let him vent and finally replied. "The LORD said to Joshua, "Stand up! What are you doing down on your face (this has nothing to do with your babbling)? Israel has sinned; they have violated my covenant, which I commanded them to keep. They have taken some of the devoted things; they have stolen, they have lied, they have put them with their own possessions. That is why the Israelites cannot stand against their enemies; they turn their backs and run because they have been made liable to destruction. I will not be with you anymore unless you destroy whatever among you is devoted to destruction."

Well! Perhaps they were so busy winning battles and collecting spoils that they disregarded God's seriousness about covenant. I can imagine that they were getting so used to battling that they failed to rehearse the covenant amongst themselves. Someone had stolen the spoil and hidden it among his own possessions as if to hide them from God. I'm sure they were only concerned about Joshua finding out.

How many of us are so concerned about what man sees that we disregard the all-knowing, all-seeing power of God? How quickly do we forget our previous victories and the reasons we got them? How do we not see patterns? Hindsight shows us the patterns and consistency of God, while foresight or keen perception uses those patterns of consistency to determine what God will do next. When you cannot see where God is going next, obey what he is telling you to do now, and his plan will be revealed.

God made it very clear that they would no longer experience victory in battle until they *un-did* what had been done to violate the covenant with God. Surely, God already knew who, what, when, where, and how this tragedy happened. He could have struck down the perpetrator just as he did Uzzah upon touching the Arc (2 Samuel 6:1-7), but let us pay attention to God's instructional strategy, and we will see that EVERYTHING is a teaching moment with God. God was grooming Joshua as a leader and had to teach him how to deal with the defeat that is caused by an insurrection in the ranks.

Joshua's first assignment is to *find it*. Find the mindset that is *devoted to destruction*. Who, in the ranks, disregards covenant? Whoever that is can be considered devoted to destruction. Leaders must pay careful attention to those who break the covenant. Marriage is a covenant, so it is a fair assessment that if a man or woman breaks his or her marital covenant, he or she cannot be trusted with the business of the Lord until sincere repentance (change of heart) happens. Covenant ties together the strings of the heart. God is in the business of covenant, and only he can determine what is in a man's heart. If a man's heart is separated from the heart of God, he becomes a potential covenant breaker and cannot be trusted to lead or fight for the Kingdom's cause.

Joshua had to find the covenant breaker and the accursed thing. All movement and mobility had stopped, and before they could expect continued victories, this thing had to be done. Leaders should never get so complacent with past victories that they fail to do what is necessary to keep winning. In this case, *removing* the hindrance was tantamount to their flow of victory. Whenever there is a breach in the flow of victories in battle, Believers must take the necessary time to search through the camps of our hearts, examine the ranks of our mindsets and very possibly check out the people we have in our circles to find the accursed thing; the thing or person that violates a covenant or is devoted to destruction.

Joshua understood the seriousness of his situation and had to move quickly, and so should we. Very often, because we are more devoted to men than we are to God, we continue to function as if there is no reason for lack of victory in our lives. We take on a mentality that accepts whatever is going on as the *"hand we were dealt."* When we do these kinds of things, it is like playing spiritual Russian Roulette with our lives and the lives of those we protect. Joshua could not afford to keep losing battles because the entire camp of God depended on those victories. He set out to *find it*.

The first instruction was to *consecrate* them. "Go, consecrate the people. Tell them, 'consecrate yourselves in preparation for tomorrow.'" Consecrate - to devote exclusively to a particular purpose. The Lord admonished Joshua to remind the people of their covenant relationships and to devote themselves and their agendas exclusively to the purpose of God. Every now and then, as Believers, we need to consecrate ourselves, our plans, and our hearts to God. We must renew and make fresh our covenant vows and re-devote our hearts to God. Not only in the time of battle but in the time of peace.

The next instruction was to have them present themselves tribe by tribe, clan by clan, family by family, and man by man, as the Lord would choose. The consequences would be dire to whoever was caught with the accursed things. He and all that belonged him to would be destroyed by fire because he had transgressed the covenant of God and wrought *folly* in Israel.

Early the next morning, As the tribes, the clans, the families, and every man came forward, certain tribes, then clans, then families were chosen until finally, the lot fell upon Achan. Some scholars say that the stone in the breast-plate of the high priest became discolored to a dullness; others say that upon questioning, the Elders made deductions as to who would be the guilty party. Either way, according to the writing of Proverbs 16:33, "The lot is cast into the lap; but the whole disposing thereof is of the Lord." Or the NLT version states, "We may throw the dice, but the Lord determines how they fall."

God's next instruction to Joshua had to be heartbreaking. Joshua had to stone it! After having been found out, Achan made a humbling confession. "It is true! I have sinned against the Lord, the God of Israel…" After locating the stolen goods, Joshua's reply to Achan was, "Why have you brought this trouble on *us?*" It is obvious by Achan's confession that he only acknowledged that he had sinned against God. He had no idea that his actions affected the entire family of God!

Sin may be concentrated in one area at a time, but it is an infection to the whole body and, therefore, must be cut out. Achan's confession was sincere but not true repentance, as he could clearly not see how the actions of one affected the whole and only after having been found out. Although it must have been devastating for Joshua to have to punish a man who was a part of the ranks and not him alone, but his entire family, it was something this leader had to do.

The instructions of God must weigh more heavily than the opinions and emotions of men. Therefore, "All Israel stoned him with stones, and burned them with fire after they had stoned them with stones." According to Numbers 15:35, stoning to death was the punishment of such offenders. Burning them after death was to show God's "utmost detestation of such persons as break forth into sins of such a public scandal or mischief." – Matthew Poole

CHAPTER 17
RE-MATCH

Joshua 8

Since the Scriptures are not necessarily novels or written as dramatically as television shows, the entire story of Achan could easily have been under-estimated in its gravity. It was indeed a drawn-out and devastating process. Although it is written and concluded in just a few verses and appears that the entire process happened in one day, please know. However, like a sit-com, the story has been greatly generalized. It was a long process to go through every tribe, every clan, and every family member. I am certain that the rumors were spreading throughout the camp, and Achan had time to repent and confess, but he did not. There was anger, sadness, and wailing throughout Israel for the men who fell in the battle of Ai and for Achan and his family, but finally, it was all over. "... So the Lord turned from the fierceness of his anger..." Joshua 7:26

God comforted Joshua and reassured him that he would be

given a re-match with Ai! Even though our failures end with loss and devastation, if we survive them, God always gives us a make-up test. After all they had recently experienced, I am pretty certain that they had learned what they needed to learn. God told Joshua that Israel would do to Ai what they did to Jericho. This is an indication that even when God is angry with us and has to exact disciplinary government, it does not mean that he has thrown us away, nor has he stripped us of our power. Once the issue is resolved, it is back to business, and we would be back on our way to victory after victory.

"Then the Lord said to Joshua, "Do not be afraid or discouraged. Take all your fighting men and attack Ai, for I have given you the king of Ai, his people, his town, and his land"

— *JOSHUA 8:1*

Once God gave Joshua the nod, he proposed a brilliant strategy. He told Joshua to set up an ambush against Ai. While 30,000 men would approach Ai in the city, the rest would lie and wait behind the city, and when Ai assumed that Israel would run away like they did before, they chased them and ran right into an ambush. At the end of the story, the city was burnt, Joshua 8:3-22, The king was taken prisoner; the inhabitants were put to the sword; the cattle and goods spoiled; the king is hanged, Joshua 8:23-29, Joshua built an altar, Joshua 8:30; offers thereon, Joshua 8:31; writes the law on stones, Joshua 8:32 It and its blessings and curses are read before the people, Joshua 8:33-35.

We can clearly see that the re-match was better for Israel

than the first fight. Not only because they were victorious, but unlike Jericho, God let them keep the spoils! The spoils were forbidden at Jericho but not at Ai. I cannot explain why, but I can see a clear message of God's grace. The re-match offered no temptation to take the forbidden and taught the people that obeying God's instructions will never leave them empty-handed.

Disobeying God's clear instructions and breaking his covenant always ends up in great suffering, but our God always gives grace to those who remain. Adam and Eve ate from the forbidden tree and suffered greatly, but they were restored and never lost their inheritance. Samson slept with the forbidden and suffered greatly, but God restored him in the end, and he still accomplished his purpose. David violated God's instructions and suffered greatly, but God restored him, and we enjoy his Psalms until this day.

Thank God for the re-match! He is truly the God of a second chance. Like Achan, there are casualties and sufferings used as life lessons, but even those tragedies are opportunities for victories in a re-match. Those who witnessed the end result of Achan's poor choice learned the possible outcome for those who disobey God's instructions. Those who learned from the *Achan lesson* enjoyed victories and spoils from season to season for years and years to come.

CHAPTER 18
LEGACY MINDED

"So Joshua took the whole land, according to all that the Lord said unto Moses; and Joshua gave it for an inheritance unto Israel according to their divisions by their tribes. And the land rested from war"

— *JOSHUA 11:23*

Legacy, according to Webster's Revised Unabridged Dictionary, is defined as a gift by will of money or personal property, a bequest; as a legacy of dishonor or disease. After some 13 grueling battles from Jericho to Hazor, Joshua and the army of Israel had finally come to a place where the *land rested from war*. No doubt, this was a welcomed reprieve. To wake up into battle after battle, year after year can take a toll on a man's mind, body and spirit, and even his faith. It is conceivable that they had fought so long and hard that many wondered whether or not the battles were even worth it or even if they would live long enough to enjoy the land for which they fought, but it was evident that God had given this land to His children as part of His legacy; his gift by will.

Those that fought continuously for the land of Canaan knew that the land was worth fighting for, even if it did not flow with milk and honey. The land would be theirs, theirs to build, theirs to cultivate, theirs to enjoy, and theirs to leave as legacies to their own children. They knew that they could not control or distribute land that was not their own. God understood the power of ownership and taught that to his children, as would any good father. Proverbs 13:22, "A good *man* leaveth an inheritance to his children's children: ..."

> *"...when your children ask in time to come, saying, 'What do these stones mean to you?' Then you shall answer them that the waters of the Jordan were cut off before the ark of the covenant of the Lord; when it crossed over the Jordan, the waters of the Jordan were cut off. And these stones shall be for a memorial to the children of Israel forever"*
>
> *— JOSHUA 4:6-7*

It is important to note that although leaving a legacy involves land, property, and things of monetary value, there is an even deeper and more meaningful purpose for legacy. Joshua instructed the children of Israel to pick up stones according to the number of the tribes of Israel and carry them on their shoulders after they passed over Jordan. These would be a symbol of their faith in God and a memorial of God's faithfulness to them. It remains an important gesture in the lives of Believer to this day.

While the stones we pick up are not physical, they are solid and lasting. Our children will not remember our faith journeys. In fact, we may work so hard at creating a legacy for them that their journeys do not resemble ours at all, but we must *take up stones* along the way. We must build a legacy of faith by sharing our faith stories with our children. We must always remind our children of God's faithfulness to us. When we leave them a monetary or tangible inheritance, we must tell them that it was all acquired as an act of God's faithfulness toward us.

This group of children would be raised in Canaan and, therefore, would not have had a wilderness experience. The only way they would know of Egyptian bondage or of a wilderness journey would be through the legacies passed down to them from generations. God has always proven to be legacy minded, as he instructed the children of Israel to honor certain days and seasons to commemorate pivotal times in their lives and to teach the children the lessons they had learned over time.

Sadly, many of these very sensitive memorials have been reduced to mere rituals and festive holidays. Very often, children will not clearly understand the meanings of such celebrations if passed down by generations who do not share the legacy along with the passion expressed when told to them by those who actually lived through it. Even more sad would be the generation of those who did not think these legacies were valuable enough to share.

Christianity is not a religion but a lifestyle and is very often remiss of stories aside from Biblical references. Testimonies have become riddled with claims of fame and dramatic prose, preaching, and teaching moments. So many Christians find themselves with something to prove *about* themselves, but legacy is about God. I get it. Every father wants to be his son's hero, and every mother wants to be a perfect example to her daughter, but we must always remember that even though our children may not experience the trials and struggles we encountered on our faith journeys, they will have some of their own. The fact that you came through what you experienced is not enough for legacy. *How* you made it through is what real legacy is made of. The truth is many of the experiences we had would have wiped us out had it not been for the help of God.

1 Samuel 7:12 says, "Then Samuel took a stone, and set it between Mizpah and Shen, and called the name of it Eben-ezer, saying, hitherto hath the Lord helped us." Placing memorial stones was one of the things Israel did after winning battles or experiencing God's divine providence. Stones are symbols of lasting memories, memories that outlive storms and turbulence. They also leave legacies for those who pass by after the storm is over. There would be people who would walk through Mizpah unharmed and unbothered by the Philistines after the slaughter there, but they would know that on that day, *the Lord thundered with a great thunder and discomfited the Philistines*; he helped the children of Israel. Their children would know that God can and will help them through the trials they face in their lifetimes.

Our children face an entirely different kind of faith fight. Such challenges as full-term abortion and same-sex marriage rights are rampant in our day. Political unrest and political correctness concepts have minimized spiritual, intrinsic values passed down through our legacies, and it makes me wonder if we have passed down the right kinds of legacies to our children. Have we passed down rules without regulation? Have we passed down contracts with unkept covenants? Have we passed down legalism without loyalty? It is important to know that legacies can be both beneficial and devastating. Surely, Achan left a legacy of what *not* to do.

The children will ask, how did this law get passed on our watch? How did our world become the world that it has become? Did someone drop the ball along the way? Even if our efforts did not change the outcomes, there should be some evidence that we tried; we fought against something; we stood for something in the name of the Lord and in the essence of spiritual legacy. Our children should know that we lived by a certain set of standards and thereby attained help from God. They should know that true legacy is a stone; it lasts longer than money or material possessions. It is solid through and through, and it will take serious manpower to uproot or bore through it. It is not a rock, a skipping chip of a stone, but a solid, impenetrable stone.

At the end of the day, the legacies of Michael Jackson, Whitney Houston, Tupac Shakur, Elvis Presley, Judy Garland, Prince, and countless others should not only include their great contributions but their tragic demises. The world would rather hide the toxic lifestyles of these great iconic figures than expose them to assure that their contributions would not be dulled by such a dark light. I get it, but what about the children who see those bright lights and become determined to *get rich or die trying*? If we only show the glitz and the glamor, the cars and the bling, the parties and the pleasures, how will the children know the dark sides of that lifestyle?

If we live *legacy-minded* lives as ambassadors or deputies on a mission, we would be more prone to live by some measure of principle. We would be prone to leaving a world for our children that may not be lined with silver and gold but stones to remind them that no matter how dark life gets for them, they have an accessible, ever-present, all-powerful, all-knowing, unseen help; Eben-ezer.

CHAPTER 19
PUT YOUR FOOT ON ITS NECK

It was no ordinary day for Joshua and the army of the Lord. "Adoni-zedek, king of Jerusalem, heard that Joshua had captured and completely destroyed Ai and killed its king, just as he had destroyed the town of Jericho and killed its king. He also learned that the Gibeonites had made peace with Israel and were now their allies. He and his people became very afraid when they heard all this because Gibeon was a large town—as large as the royal cities and larger than Ai. And the Gibeonite men were strong warriors.

So, King Adoni-zedek of Jerusalem sent messengers to several other kings: Hoham of Hebron, Piram of Jarmuth, Japhia of Lachish, and Debir of Eglon. "Come and help me destroy Gibeon," he urged them, "for they have made peace with Joshua and the people of Israel." So these five Amorite kings combined their armies for a united attack. They moved all their troops into place and attacked Gibeon" (Joshua 10:1-3 NLT).

After the re-match in Ai, five kings came together against them, and it looked like a slaughter in the making, but God assured Joshua that they would have victory. "Do not be afraid of them," the LORD said to Joshua, "for I have given you victory over them. Not a single one of them will be able to stand up to you" (Joshua 10:12). They were already assured a win, but Joshua prayed a ridiculous prayer, and God gave them a ridiculous victory. "On the day the LORD gave the Israelites victory over the Amorites, Joshua prayed to the LORD in front of all the people of Israel. He said, "Let the sun stand still over Gibeon and the moon over the valley of Aijalon. So, the sun stood still, and the moon stayed in place until the nation of Israel had defeated its enemies" (Joshua 10:13, NLT).

In the heat of a battle, when it feels like your enemies have all gathered together against you, try praying a ridiculous prayer! Sometimes you want a crazy victory; you want to see God do something in a crazy way. Have you ever had a thirst for something supernatural? Joshua prayed a prayer for results that he could take absolutely no credit for. It was clear that Joshua did not intend to claim this victory for himself. He already knew they would win the battle, but now he wanted the people to see God, be God.

It is important to win battles, but it is more important to share that those battles were only won with the help of almighty God. The children of Israel needed to see it, and more importantly, their enemies needed to see it. When Joshua and the spies went to Rahab's house, she told them that the reputation of their God caused the men of those nations' hearts to melt in fear. This was very important for them to hear because to know that God's reputation preceded them meant that God would protect his name and his legacy. They would know that the battle was not only theirs, but God's, and they would be victorious.

During the battle, the five kings escaped and hid in a cave at Makkedah. When Joshua heard that they had been found, he issued this command: "Cover the opening of the cave with large rocks and place guards at the entrance to keep the kings inside. The rest of you continue chasing the enemy and cut them down from the rear. Don't give them a chance to get back to their towns, for the LORD your God has given you victory over them" (Joshua 10:18).

"So, Joshua and the Israelite army continued the slaughter and completely crushed the enemy. They totally wiped out the five armies except for a tiny remnant that managed to reach their fortified towns. Then the Israelites returned safely to Joshua in the camp at Makkedah. After that, no one dared to speak even a word against Israel" (Joshua 10:20,21, NLT).

Then Joshua said, "Remove the rocks covering the opening of the cave, and bring the five kings to me." So they brought the five kings out of the cave—the kings of Jerusalem, Hebron, Jarmuth, Lachish, and Eglon. When they brought them out, Joshua told the commanders of his army, "Come and put your feet on the kings' necks." And they did as they were told" (Joshua 10:24).

Having the inferior rank put their feet on the necks of the superior is a common oriental practice done to humble and humiliate their enemies and to show superior dominance. In this case, Joshua says, "Don't ever be afraid or discouraged," Joshua told his men. "Be strong and courageous, for the LORD is going to do this to all of your enemies." This act was intended to show the superior dominance of God.

As Believers, we must always give glory to God as the superior being. Although there are varying perspectives of the *foot on the neck* concept, it must all end in the glory of God. Israel's enemies were both angry and disappointed. They were confused because they were five nations against one, and technically, they should have won this battle. Although Joshua's keen military skill and Israel's unmatched might played a part in this victory, it was God's obvious intervention that ultimately brought them victory.

Israel's perspective of the *foot on the neck* is that God would continually *hold them down* or have their backs. God would always defend them and keep their enemies under their feet. It is important that they know they would still have to fight, but as long as they remained in a right relationship with God, those fights are fixed.

CHAPTER 20
A WINNER'S HEART

"If you don't want me to win, you shouldn't let me play; I play to win!"

— CYNTHIA MCINNIS

Everyone wants to be a winner but to always win. You need more than a *want to*. You need a winner's heart. A winner's heart governs a winner's moves and causes an individual to proceed at all times with winning on his mind. A winner's heart does not compete for prizes or trinkets. It's the win that thrills them.

It is important to know what an opponent determines to be a win. Not every win is tangible. Not every win can be determined by some judge. For example, when a person defies his own limitations, he may consider that to be a win. When a person does his very best, regardless of any proposed outcome, he determines that to be a win. When what he does works for him and/or benefits others, he considers that to be a win.

There are so many winners in the Bible but only a few who actually have, what I deem, a winner's heart. Walk with me as I call out one of my favorites and conclude with the major protagonist in this book, Joshua.

"I have fought a good fight, I have finished my course, I have kept the faith. Henceforth there is laid up for me a crown of righteousness, which the Lord, the righteous judge, shall give me at that day:..." (2 Timothy 4:7-8). If hearts could speak, this would be the verbiage that expresses the three-fold cord of a winner's heart! At the end of his life, Paul wrote this moving letter to his protégé, Timothy. Paul uses the terms *fought a good fight* and *finished my course* that metaphorically relate to a physical race or sporting event. It is not new to him, as he mentioned finishing his course in Acts 2:24. It is obvious that to Paul, the win was the sum total of these three things; fighting a good fight, finishing his course, and keeping the faith. These were his greatest challenges.

Fighting a good fight could very well mean fighting a clean, honest, and fair fight, following the rules of the match, and doing his very best. In a modern-day bout, these things alone never determine a win, but for Paul, it was part of his win. It is easy to cheat, especially when things get difficult. So many make excuses in the thick of the fight when things get painful or discouraging. We digress from the rules and hide our faces, blocking punches and painful experiences. Real fighters go into the rink knowing that getting hit is a part of the package. Every fighter must prepare for his fight, both physically and mentally.

PURSUING DESTINY AGAINST THE ODDS

In the case of the Believer, the weapons of our warfare are never carnal but those that spiritually equip us for a life that is often represented as one of conflict. "That noble conflict with sin, the world, the flesh, and the devil, Paul now says he had been able to maintain." – Barnes

Paul shows us how to fight a good fight as he encouraged Timothy to do in 1 Timothy 6:12. He wrote a full description in Ephesians 6:10-18. He followed his own instructions, and at the close of his life, he pronounced, I have fought a good fight.

I once heard Dr. Myles Monroe say that people who know their purpose in life and have finished it do not fear death; they actually welcome it. He used Paul's own words in 2 Timothy 4:6, "For I am now ready to be offered, and the time of my departure is at hand." Paul says the second cord of his defining win is that he had *finished* his course. He knew his purpose, as described by *his course*. Finishing what you have been called to do is definitely a win. It's similar to a marathon where winners need only to finish the course to win. It doesn't matter whether you finish first or last. As long as you finish, you win.

People who do not know their life's purpose will never welcome death. They are always unfulfilled and seeking more, stopping and starting, trying to finish what they started last. The key is to use the energy to be sure of your calling, not just trying to accomplish *things*. "Wherefore the rather, brethren, give diligence to make your calling and election sure: for if ye do these things, ye shall never fail" (2 Peter 1:10).

How many of us spend a lifetime just doing different things to get more and more money, more and more fame, and more and more things, but never fulfill our life's purpose? Monroe says Jesus never considered what he did a job, but his *work*. "I must work the works of him that sent me, while it is day: the night cometh, when no man can work" (John 9:4). A job is what finances you, but your work is what fulfills you. You can get fired from a job, but you can never be removed from your work, finally, he says, a job is what you do, but your work is your purpose. If you seek out your purpose, do it, and finish it …you win!

Finally, Paul says, what is the ultimate part of the three-cord win - I have kept the faith. "I have steadfastly maintained the faith of the gospel; or, have lived a life of fidelity to my Master. Probably the expression means that he had kept his plighted faith to the Redeemer, or had spent a life in faithfully endeavoring to serve the Lord."- Barnes

What a personal goal! What an internally gratifying testimony! This is not a win for the shelf-life or a win for the roar of the crowd; this is the voice of a personal win. Keeping the faith does not mean never having doubted but rather, turning those doubts around permanently by your faith. Keeping the faith does not mean hollering when it hurts but instead hollering when it hurts without quitting. Keeping the faith does not mean feeling sad or even depressed when the weight of life's pressures lay down on your shoulders. You should use your faith to get out of that state.

It was Paul that told us how to get the kind of faith required to turn any doubtful situation around in Romans 10:17, "So then faith cometh by hearing, and hearing by the word of God." It is this third part of the three-fold cord of the winner's heart that caused Paul to do the first two. It takes faith to fight a good fight and finish one's course.

While we are inundated with daily living activities, religious practices, community services, one self-improvement, professional development task after the other, it is most wise to stop and study God's word. This is where you will undoubtedly find your life's purpose and how to carry it out. The word of God tells us in Proverbs 3:6, "In all thy ways acknowledge him, and he shall direct thy paths." This, by far, is one of the most essential directives in the Bible. It will save us many wasted years and many painful life lessons, but it is easier said than done; it takes practice and sincere devotion. Adherence to this instruction is worth every sacrifice because it will ultimately lead you to your life's purpose and teach you how to do it and finish it.

Joshua did not know his purpose at the beginning of his life. It was not until God strategically placed him with Moses, and he became Moses's servant. He became a leader while serving. Not knowing the fate of Israel, when leaving Egypt, he *never left the tent* of his mentor. He served Moses unselfishly, not knowing he was being prepared for his life's purpose.

Having never fought a battle before this, Joshua was summoned to a battle with Amelek by his mentor Moses'. His obvious love and respect for Moses's gave him the desire to win and began the development of a *winner's heart*. The win began in his heart and was won with his hands. His love and respect for God, coupled with that for his mentor, made Joshua an unstoppable force throughout his entire life.

After the death of Moses, Joshua became the leader of Israel. Against overwhelming odds, Joshua led the Israelite army in its conquest of the Promised Land. He apportioned the land to the tribes and governed them for a time. Without a doubt, Joshua's greatest accomplishment in life was his unwavering loyalty and faith in God. Battle after battle, victory after victory, through short-lived failures and fewer defeats, Joshua remained faithful to his purpose. He fought a good fight, he finished his course, and he kept the faith. He is by far one of the greatest examples of one who examples the task of pursuing destiny against the odds.

Made in the USA
Middletown, DE
07 July 2023